LORRAINE KELLY'S BABY & TODDLER EATING PLAN

LORRAINE KELLY'S BABY & TODDLER EATING PLAN

OVER 100 HEALTHY, QUICK & EASY RECIPES

LORRAINE KELLY WITH ANITA BEAN

This edition published in Great Britain in 2004 by
Virgin Books Ltd, Thames Wharf Studios, Rainville Road, London W6 9HA

First published in 2002 by Virgin Books Ltd

Reprinted 2005 (twice)

A catalogue record for the book is available
from the British Library.

ISBN 0 7535 0869 9

Designed by Smith & Gilmour

Printed and bound in Great Britain by Mackays of Chatham

Contents

Introduction

It was only when I discovered I was to be a mother that I really started thinking seriously about food – for me and for the baby growing inside me.

Like so many women I have been on daft diets since I was about 16 and, while I could tell you exactly how many calories were in an apple, I had no idea how to make an apple pie. At school I was taught maths and chemistry – but never received any lessons in how to make vegetable soup or how to make mashed potatoes.

My mum is a really good cook, but I was never interested in learning what she was up to in the kitchen – I was either studying for my exams, or out with my friends. When I did move into a flat of my own, I would occasionally call her saying things like 'I've bought a cabbage, what do I do with it?' My culinary expertise consisted of a pretty good spag bog and . . . well that was about it really.

When I was single and working as a TV reporter and on call 24 hours a day, I would just grab food when I could – take-aways, microwave meals and bags of crisps. There was dust on my cooker and a huge gap in my education. My husband, Steve, who has looked after himself since he was 16, is an excellent cook. While I would happily just have some toast and beans for dinner, he will cook himself meat, two veg and all the trimmings and he can knock up a curry to die for. I was happy to let him do most of the cooking, while I opened the wine and did the clearing up.

But that all changed when I found out I was pregnant. I realised that it was vitally important that I ate a proper diet and took care of myself. I had an insatiable craving for tinned mandarins, but I was very specific about the kind I needed. I didn't want the kind in syrup or sugar – they had to be those sour tinned ones in their own juice. Poor Steve cleaned out most of the supermarkets in our area. I can't even look at them now, but back then I could polish off ten bowls in one sitting.

I put on an awful lot of weight when I was pregnant, mainly because, although I was eating reasonably healthily, I was consuming enormous quantities of food, and I wasn't doing any real exercise. At that time I was presenting the much earlier slot on GMTV with Eamonn. The alarm would go off at four o'clock in the morning. I would haul myself out of bed, which got increasingly more difficult as I grew bigger and bigger, and by the end of that morning's show I was ready for my bed again. Anyone who does shift work suffers from tiredness and I am sure any nurses or factory workers doing unsociable hours while pregnant know only too well just how exhausting it can be. Of course, I should have gone for a walk or a swim, but instead I went for an afternoon nap with a chocolate orange and a good book. I remember my pregnancy, especially towards the last few months, consisted of going to work, going to bed and eating a lot.

Once I had my daughter Rosie, I still needed to eat properly because I wanted to breast feed. I was incredibly lucky as she took to breast feeding right away and I didn't really have to do anything other than just supply the grub on demand. I know some women simply can't manage to breast feed, but there really is no better start for your baby – and it is much easier than faffing about with bottles and baby milk and sterilising machines.

Of course, because I was feeding, I continued to eat King Kong-sized portions and so it took me a while to get back into shape, but when Rosie started on solid food, I felt I could then go on a programme to get my old figure back. I hate the word diet and I firmly believe that diets make you fat – so I went on a healthy eating plan combined with a bit of walking and managed to get back to a reasonable size.

It really is a big responsibility to make sure that your children eat well and eat healthily. What you feed them will affect their health;

habits they pick up when they are tiny will stay with them for ever. You want your child to grow up strong and full of health and happiness and one way you can ensure this happens is by making sure you give them the best possible food.

As parents we shape and influence our children's attitude to food. If you are always on a faddy diet or glowering at a lettuce leaf, your daughter will pick that up, even at a very early age. Not only do we have to be sensible about what we give our children to eat but we must also be conscious of the messages that we send out about food. Like many of you reading this book, I am a working mum and I simply do not have the time to cook complicated meals that take lots of time and effort. You don't have to have a degree in food technology or become a prisoner in the kitchen to be sure of giving your child good, healthy meals that are quick and easy to prepare and that you won't feel guilty about putting down in front of them. And don't beat yourself up about serving chicken nuggets and chips now and again – or taking them for a pizza. Just so long as they aren't living constantly on a diet of fast food take-aways. There really isn't much point in banning sweeties and chocolate. By doing that you will just make them even more desirable. Children adore sweets and you just have to be sensible about when and how you dole them out. I can always recognise the children who aren't allowed cake or sugar when they come to visit as they always sneakily empty the biscuit tin.

I want you to use this book to make your life easier and to make sure your child is getting a healthy and balanced diet. The recipes are all tried and tested and were firm favourites with my daughter and her friends as they were growing up. I know that cooking meals for your family can be a bit of an unrewarding slog – which is why I want to make it as stress free and enjoyable as possible.

Chapter 1
What is a Balanced Diet?

To grow up healthy and strong, children need to eat a balanced diet. This means they need to get all the essential nutrients – protein, carbohydrate, fat, vitamins, minerals and water – in the right proportions. Eating a balanced diet is all about eating a wide variety of foods. The easiest way to plan your child's diet is by using the Food Guide Pyramid on page 11.

The foods at the bottom of the pyramid – cereals, bread, pasta, potatoes – should make up the biggest proportion of your toddler's diet while those at the top – fats and sugary foods – should be eaten in smaller amounts. There are no forbidden foods – the key is moderation.

• Provide foods from each group every day
• Include a variety of foods from each group
• Aim to have the recommended number of portions from each group each day

Grains and potatoes
6 portions a day
This group includes bread, cereal, rice, pasta and potatoes and should make up the largest part of your child's diet. These foods are major sources of energy (as complex carbohydrates) and also supply fibre, B vitamins and minerals.

Try to include mostly wholegrain or unrefined cereals in your child's diet – wholemeal bread, porridge, wholegrain breakfast cereals and wholewheat pasta. These are richer in iron, vitamins and fibre than white or refined varieties.

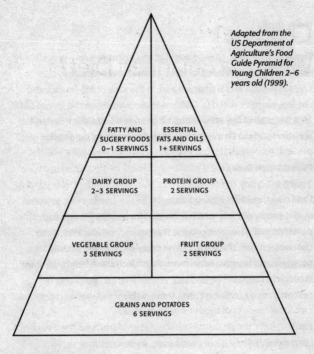

Adapted from the US Department of Agriculture's Food Guide Pyramid for Young Children 2–6 years old (1999).

FATTY AND SUGERY FOODS
0–1 SERVINGS

ESSENTIAL FATS AND OILS
1+ SERVINGS

DAIRY GROUP
2–3 SERVINGS

PROTEIN GROUP
2 SERVINGS

VEGETABLE GROUP
3 SERVINGS

FRUIT GROUP
2 SERVINGS

GRAINS AND POTATOES
6 SERVINGS

Vegetables and fruit

3 portions of vegetables a day
2 portions of fruit a day

Fruit and vegetables provide vitamins, minerals, fibre and a group of compounds called phytochemicals, which help to boost immunity and protect the body from cancer and heart disease. Different fruit and vegetables contain different nutrients so provide as much variety as possible. Aim for a mix of colours: orange/ yellow (carrots, apricots, mangoes), red (tomatoes, red peppers, strawberries), green (broccoli, peas, spinach), purple (grapes, blackberries), white (apples, pears, cauliflower).

Dairy foods
2–3 portions a day
These foods – milk, cheese, yoghurt and fromage frais – provide calcium, which is needed for strong bones and teeth. They also contain protein and B vitamins and, in the case of full-fat milk and cheese, vitamins A and D. Children under two should be given full-fat milk because of the extra calories it provides. Semi-skimmed milk is suitable for children over two provided they are eating a varied diet.

Protein-rich foods
2 portions a day
Lean meat, chicken, turkey, fish, eggs, beans, lentils, nuts, soya and quorn supply protein, which is needed for healthy growth and development. They also provide B vitamins, iron and zinc. Try to choose lean cuts of meat and limit processed meats, such as sausages and burgers, to no more than twice a week because they are high in saturated fat and salt. Vegetarians can get plenty of protein from eggs, pulses, nuts, tofu and quorn as well as dairy foods.

Tip
Even if your family is not vegetarian, try to introduce some vegetable protein foods such as beans, lentils and soya products into your children's diet. These foods provide a unique type of fibre that's particularly beneficial for the digestive system, as well as lots of important minerals and phytochemicals not found in animal proteins.

Essential fats and oils
1 portion a day
Foods rich in essential fats include nuts, seeds, rapeseed oil, olive oil, sunflower oil and oily fish. These can easily be included in your child's diet in the form of spreads and oils used in cooking (casseroles, soups, one pot meals, Bolognese sauce, etc.). Try to give oily fish, such as sardines, salmon or mackerel at least once a week.

Fatty and sugary foods

Maximum 1 portion a day

This group includes biscuits, chocolate bars, cakes, puddings, soft drinks and sweets. These foods supply few essential nutrients yet lots of calories ('empty calories') so they should be eaten only in moderation. Added sugars should only be used for enhancing the flavour of healthy foods (e.g. jam on toast or sugar on porridge), or making acidic foods palatable (e.g. with cooking apples for apple crumble).

How big is a portion?

The portion sizes opposite are a rough guide. Children's needs vary so be guided by your own child's appetite. One- to two-year-olds need the same variety and number of servings as older toddlers but may need fewer calories. Offer them smaller amounts.

MY CHILD WON'T EAT VEGETABLES!

It is often a struggle to get young children to eat the recommended three portions of fruit and vegetables. Here are some ideas for encouraging your toddler to eat more vegetables.

- Toddlers who refuse most vegetables will often eat raw or lightly cooked 'finger' vegetables, such as carrot sticks, pepper strips, cherry tomatoes, sugar-snap peas, baby sweetcorn or cucumber sticks – try dunking in a dip e.g. hummus (recipe page 114).

- Add a handful of chopped broccoli, peppers, courgettes or mushrooms to pasta sauces – purée or mash if necessary

- Hide vegetables (e.g. carrots, mushrooms, spinach) in Bolognese sauce, in soups, lasagnes, stews, bakes and pies

- Make vegetables more fun – arrange broccoli and cauliflower as trees on a base of mashed potato; make faces (e.g. use carrots for eyes, baby corn for a nose, red peppers for the mouth, broccoli for hair, or whatever else your child likes!)

- Let your toddler decorate his or her own pizzas with a selection of peppers, mushrooms, tomatoes and pineapple

- Fruit has similar nutrient to vegetables so is a good substitute

APPROXIMATE DAILY NEEDS OF CHILDREN BETWEEN ONE AND THREE YEARS

Food Group	Number of portions each day	Food	Portion size (1–2 Years)	Portion size (2–3 Years)
Grains and Potatoes	6	Bread	½ slice	1 small slice
		Rolls/muffins	½ roll	½–1 roll
		Pasta/rice	1–2 tablespoons	2 tablespoons
		Breakfast cereal	1–2 tablespoons	2 tablespoons
		Porridge	1–2 tablespoons	2 tablespoons
		Potatoes, sweet potatoes, yams	½ potato (walnut sized)	1 small potato (Egg-sized)
Vegetables	3	Broccoli, cauliflower	1 spear/floret	1–2 spears/florets
		Carrots	½ carrot	1 small carrot
		Peas	1 tablespoon	1–2 tablespoons
		Other vegetables	1 tablespoon	1–2 tablespoons

Category		Food		
Fruit	2	Apple, pear, peach, banana	½ fruit	½–1 fruit
		Plum, kiwi fruit, apricot	½–1 fruit	1 fruit
		Strawberries, raspberries	1 tablespoon	1–2 tablespoons
Dairy	2–3	Milk	1 cup	1 cup
		Cheese	40 g (1½ oz)	40 g (1½ oz)
		Yoghurt/fromage frais	1–2 pots	1–2 pots
Protein-rich foods	2	Lean meat	½ slice/30g (1 oz)	½–1 slice/40g (1½ oz)
		Poultry/fish	30g (1 oz)	40g (1½ oz)
		Egg	½	½–1
		Lentils/beans	1 tablespoon	1–2 tablespoons
		Tofu/soya burger or sausage	½	½–1
Essential fats and oils	1	Nuts and seeds	1–2 teaspoons	1 tablespoon
		Seed oils, nut oils	2 teaspoons	1 tablespoon
		Oily fish*	60 g (2 oz)	60 g (2 oz)

*Oily fish is very rich in essential fats so just one portion a week would cover a toddler's daily needs

NUTRITION GUIDE

Carbohydrates

Carbohydrates are the major dietary source of energy. There are two main types: simple carbohydrates (sugars) and complex carbohydrates (starch and fibre). Both types are turned into glucose in the body, which is then used for energy.

Some types of carbohydrate – sugary foods, soft drinks, biscuits, white bread – are turned into glucose very rapidly producing a short-lived energy 'high' followed by an energy 'low'. So, these carbohydrate foods should be eaten only in moderation.

By contrast, most complex carbohydrate foods – wholegrain bread and cereals as well as fruit, beans and lentils – release energy slowly over a longer period. So, these foods will give children longer lasting energy and should form the main part of their diet.

These foods are also richer in vitamins, minerals and fibre than refined carbohydrate foods, which have had much of their nutritional value removed during processing.

HOW MUCH FIBRE SHOULD CHILDREN HAVE?

Fibre is important for young children as it helps their digestive system work properly, prevents constipation and keeps them 'regular'. Unrefined foods naturally rich in fibre – wholemeal bread, wholegrain cereals, pulses, fruit, and vegetables – are also rich in vitamins and minerals. But they can be quite filling for small appetites so don't expect your child to eat big portions. Bran-enriched cereals are not a good idea for young children as they are particularly filling and may mean that your child cannot eat enough to meet his or her calorie needs.

Protein

Protein is needed for growth and development. It is the building block of all cells in the body and makes up a large portion of children's muscles, organs, skin and hair. It is also needed for making enzymes, hormones and antibodies. Children need more protein relative to their size than adults so it is important that they

get two portions of protein rich foods daily – lean meat, poultry,
fish, pulses, eggs, nuts, tofu and quorn (see Food Guide Pyramid,
page 11) – as well as two portions of dairy products.

Proteins are made up of amino acids. Nine of these must be
provided by the diet (the 'essential amino acids'), while the body
can make the rest. For the body to use food proteins properly, all
nine essential amino acids have to be present. Animal proteins
as well as soya and quorn contain a good balance of the nine
essential amino acids. But plant proteins (pulses, cereals, nuts)
contain smaller amounts so these need to be combined together
(e.g. beans on toast; lentils and rice; peanut butter on bread) to
make a full complement of amino acids. The general rule of thumb
is to have grains and pulses or nuts and grains together.

Fat

Fat forms a more important part of children's diets than adults'.
It supplies energy, which helps support their growth and
development as well as fuelling their physical activity. While many
adults try to reduce the amount of fat in their diet, this principle
should not be applied to young children who need the extra calories
provided by fat for growth. A low-fat diet could result in malnutrition.

Fat is also needed to help the body absorb and use the fat-soluble
vitamins, A, D and E. Finally, certain types of fats – the essential fatty
acids – are crucial for good health and immunity.

Fats Explained

There are two main types of fat: saturated and unsaturated fats.
Although saturated are generally considered 'bad' and unsaturated
the key to good health is to provide the right balance of different fats.
Saturated fats are found in meat and full-fat dairy products as well
as margarine, biscuits and desserts made with palm oil (a highly
saturated fat). High intakes of these fats are harmful because they
can raise blood cholesterol levels both in children and adults.
Introduce healthy eating by choosing lean meat and by giving

children biscuits, puddings and cakes only in moderation. *Mono-unsaturated fats* are found in olive oil, rapeseed oil, avocados and nuts. Polyunsaturated fats are found in sunflower oil and many vegetable oil margarines. Both types help lower blood cholesterol levels but the monounsaturated fats offer the greatest protection against heart disease. Choose olive oil and rapeseed oil for cooking whenever you can (see recipes).

The essential fats have to be supplied by the diet because, unlike other fats, they cannot be made in the body. The two main families of essential fatty acids are omega-3 and omega-6. Both are important for brain and visual development, as well as making hormones and keeping the immune system healthy. But it is the omega-3 fatty acids, found in oily fish (sardines, mackerel, salmon), rapeseed oil, walnuts, sweet potatoes, omega-3 enriched eggs and pumpkin seeds, that are often lacking in children's (and adults') diets causing an imbalance of fatty acids in the body. Omega-6 fatty acids are easier to find – most vegetable oils, nuts and seeds. Try to get the right balance by including oily fish at least once a week in your family's diet or including one other good source of omega-3s daily.

Finally, there is one other type of fat that you need to be aware of: trans fats. These are particularly harmful fats, which are formed during the commercial process of hydrogenation. When liquid oils are converted into hardened hydrogenated fats by heating to very high temperatures with hydrogen, some of the fat molecules become chemically altered, and turn into trans fats. These trans fats are bad for health because they push up blood cholesterol levels and increase heart disease risk. Many experts believe that trans fats are even more harmful than saturated fats and should be avoided whenever possible. Unfortunately many foods contain hydrogenated fats and partially hydrogenated fats – margarine, low fat spread, biscuits, cakes, ice-cream, cereal bars, desserts, crackers – which makes it difficult to avoid them altogether. Try to keep these processed foods to a sensible minimum.

Vitamins and minerals

Vitamins and minerals are needed in much smaller amounts than carbohydrate, protein or fat but are just as essential for good health. Vitamins support the immune system, help the brain function properly and help convert food into energy. They are important for healthy skin and hair, controlling growth and balancing hormones. Some vitamins – the B vitamins and vitamin C – must be provided by the diet each day, as they cannot be stored.

Minerals are needed for other essential functions, including bone strength, haemoglobin manufacture, fluid balance and muscle contraction.

Children should be able to get their daily vitamin and mineral needs from their food. Help them eat a balanced diet by using the Food Guide Pyramid and encourage them to eat a wide variety of foods from each group. Children who eat a restricted range of foods are unlikely to be meeting their vitamin and mineral needs so they may benefit from a vitamin supplement (see below).

Do children need supplements?

Children who eat a varied, balanced diet probably don't need to take extra vitamins.

But few children manage to do this and many parents worry that their children may not be getting enough. Government guidelines recommend breast-fed babies over six months and children under five years should be given vitamin drops containing vitamins A, C, and D (see 'Vitamin Drops', page 74). But if your toddler is going through a phase of food refusal or fussy eating, it may be a good idea to give a simple children's supplement containing a broader range of vitamins and minerals. Choose one that is formulated for your child's age and stick to the dose recommended on the label. Speak to your health visitor or to a qualified nutritionist or dietitian if you suspect a deficiency.

Phytochemicals

Phytochemicals are compounds found naturally in plants. Many are powerful antioxidants that work with vitamins and minerals to protect the body from degenerative diseases (such as heart disease and cancer), boost immunity and fight harmful bacteria and viruses. There are hundreds of different types of phytochemicals and the best way to make sure your children gets them is to include at least five portions of fruits and vegetables in their diet.

Encourage children to eat a wide variety of different coloured foods:

- Green – Broccoli, cabbage, Brussels sprouts, curly kale, spinach
- Red/purple – Plums, aubergines, cherries, red grapes, strawberries, blackberries, blueberries, tomatoes
- Yellow/orange – Peaches, apricots, nectarines, oranges, yellow peppers, butternut squash
- White/yellow – Onions, garlic, apples, pears, celery
- Brown/green – Beans, lentils, nuts, seeds

ABOUT THE RECIPES

In the following chapters I suggest a detailed menu planner and recipes for each stage of your child's development up to the time when he or she can eat more or less the same things as you. Remember that they are meant to be a guide to help you, not a rigid plan that you must stick to at all costs. Be guided by your own instincts and your child's appetite.

Measures

The quantities of ingredients in the recipes are intended as a guide. Adapt the amount to suit your baby's or toddler's tastes. For example, your baby may prefer a little more cauliflower or a little less broccoli in the Spring Vegetable Medley Recipe on page 63.

I have kept the recipes as straightforward as possible, using everyday measures such as one carrot or a handful of peas rather than expecting you to weigh all your fruit and vegetables. Here is a guide to the average weights used in the recipes.

1 potato = 150g (5 oz)   1 parsnip = 125g (4 oz)

1 sweet potato = 175g (6 oz) 1 handful peas = 30g (1 oz)

1 carrot = approx 60g (2 oz)   1 floret of broccoli/cauliflower = 30g (1 oz)

Portions

Suggested portion sizes are approximate. All babies and toddlers have different appetites. Your baby may eat only one or two teaspoons at first so store the remainder in the fridge or freezer.

Toddler Recipes

After the age of one year your child can eat the same food as the rest of the family. The quantities given in the recipes serve two adults and two young children but you can increase or decrease the quantities depending on the number of servings you need.

Presentation

After the age of 9 months, the way you present your child's food becomes more important. Many young children find large platefuls of food off putting so offer them small portions rather than risk them refusing the whole meal. To encourage your toddler to eat the meal, try arranging the food in a simple pattern or an interesting shape – a star or a funny face work well. There's no need to create a culinary masterpiece at every meal (despite what other well-meaning cookery books may advise!). Most of the time, it's enough to present different foods in individual piles. Try to choose different coloured and textured foods.

Home-made vegetable stock

A number of the recipes include vegetable stock. Don't use stock cubes, granules or powder until your baby is at least 9 months old because they contain a lot of salt. This can place a strain on your baby's kidneys and encourage a taste for salty food rather than an appreciation of the natural flavours of the food. Use either a ready made no-salt stock or use the following recipe to make your own. Vegetable stock cubes or Swiss vegetable bouillon powder can be used in the toddler recipes. Use the low-salt version if it is available in your supermarket.

900 ml (1½ pints) water	**1 onion, roughly chopped**
2 carrots, roughly sliced	**2 celery sticks, halved**
1 leek, halved	**2 bay leaves**
2 sprigs of thyme	**2 sprigs of parsley**

Put the water, vegetables and herbs in a large saucepan.

Bring to the boil and simmer gently for at least 45 minutes. Leave to cool and then strain, discarding the vegetables and herbs.

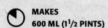 **MAKES**
600 ML (1½ PINTS)

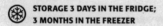 **STORAGE 3 DAYS IN THE FRIDGE;**
3 MONTHS IN THE FREEZER

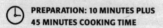 **PREPARATION: 10 MINUTES PLUS**
45 MINUTES COOKING TIME

PART ONE
FEEDING YOUR BABY

Chapter 2
From Four Months

For the first four to six months, breast or formula milk provides everything your baby needs. After this time, your baby will need more calories and nutrients in order to carry on growing properly and keep healthy. This is the time to introduce solids. Weaning – moving on to a mixed diet – represents a big milestone in your baby's development.

Weaning should be a gradual process. For the first two months, the aim is just to get your baby used to, and enjoying, taking food from a spoon as well as introducing him or her to different tastes and textures. Remember, breast milk or formula is your baby's main food.

WHEN TO START WEANING

There are no hard and fast rules but most babies are ready for their first tastes of solid food between four and six months. Don't be tempted to offer solids any earlier even if your baby seems to have a big appetite. Many mums offer solids in the hope that their baby will sleep longer through the night but babies need frequent feeds and there's nothing you can do about that at this stage! Apart from the fact that babies don't need anything other than milk for the first four months, they are physically unable to manage solids. They still have the natural tongue-thrust reflex, which makes them push food back out of their mouths so they cannot 'eat' food anyway. Before four months, babies cannot sit upright enough to feed properly yet and their digestive systems and kidneys are not mature enough to cope with anything other than milk. There is also the danger of allergy and possibly obesity later on if solids are introduced too early.

On the other hand, your baby should be on solids by six months. By then, milk is no longer enough to satisfy babies' nutritional needs.

How to tell whether your baby is ready for weaning
- Your baby starts demanding more frequent feeds
- Your baby wakes in the night for an extra feed when previously she slept through
- Your baby still seems hungry after a milk feed
- Your baby shows an interest in your food

HOW TO BEGIN

Choose one regular mealtime, ideally when your baby is most hungry. You will need to give your baby your full attention and allow plenty of time, so choose a quiet time of day when both of you are relaxed, perhaps midday. Sit your baby on your lap or in a baby car seat or bouncing chair, whichever feels most natural. Arm yourself with a weaning spoon and large absorbent bib to protect your baby's clothes. Start with a little of your baby's usual milk to take the edge off his or her appetite. Then offer a small amount of purée on the end of a spoon. Finish with the rest of the milk feed.

If your baby is keen, you can offer one or two teaspoons, gradually increasing the amount each day. Increase the amount gradually over a few days to five or six teaspoons. Be guided by your baby's appetite. You'll know how much to give because babies will turn their heads away when they have had enough. After one or two weeks once feeding is going well, you can introduce a second meal, say at breakfast time (see Meal Planner, page 31).

When your baby says no!
Some babies eat what is offered straight away, others will turn their heads away and refuse to open their mouths. Don't worry if your baby doesn't seem interested in solids at first. It's a very new experience and it may take several attempts before you manage to get anything into your baby's mouth. Most babies swallow a little food and dribble the rest down their chins! If your baby seems upset or refuses to take solids, don't persist – try again in a few days' time. If your baby is teething or unwell, he or she may not be interested in solid food. Continue with the usual milk feeds for a while.

FIRST FOODS

Baby rice
Baby rice mixed with a little of your baby's usual milk is a good first food. It should be quite runny to start with – about the consistency of cream – but just thick enough to be easily sucked from a spoon. You can buy packets of baby rice from supermarkets and chemists.

Purées
Next try puréed root vegetables, such as potato or swede, and fruit, such as apple or pear. To start with, give single purées – plain or diluted with a little baby rice and expressed breast or formula milk to introduce the flavours gradually. After two to four weeks, you can combine two or more foods.

Avoid sugar and salt
Don't add sugar or salt to your baby's food even if it tastes bland to you. Babies' kidneys can't cope with salt and their digestive systems cannot cope with added sugar at this stage.

TAKE IT EASY

Please, please remember that weaning your baby isn't a competition.

It really doesn't matter if your mum tells you that you were weaned at three months, or that all your friends are feeding their babies solid food and your baby is still just drinking milk. It is all about what is right for your baby. Listen to your baby. She will soon let you know whether milk alone is just not enough.

We started Rosie on a teeny bit of baby rice milk with breast milk when she was nearly five months old. It was a big occasion and, of course, proud dad was there to video her every expression and to send the tapes up to the grannies.

Be warned – weaning can be a very messy business. Try not to worry about spilt food on the kitchen floor. Put down newspapers or plastic sheets and be prepared for a goo-covered baby. You will probably end up splattered as well – so wear your oldest track suit.

Do not add any other food, such as baby cereal, to your baby's bottle because of the risk of choking. It doesn't teach your baby about new tastes or textures or how to chew.

Is organic food better for babies?

Expert opinion differs as to whether organic food is more nutritious than non-organic. Some studies show that organic fruit and vegetables have a higher content of certain vitamins and minerals but the difference isn't huge.

Many believe that organic foods are safer because they contain no (or at least only trace amounts of) contaminants such as pesticides, antibiotics and nitrates. Commercial organic baby food is free from artificial additives, unhealthy hydrogenated fats (see Chapter 1, page 17) and GM ingredients.

Unfortunately, many organic foods are a lot more expensive, which puts many people off buying them regularly. It is more important that you choose good quality fresh produce whether organic or not.

SUITABLE FIRST FOODS FROM FOUR MONTHS

Foods to Include

Serve as smooth runny purées:

Non-wheat cereal such as baby rice or polenta (cornmeal)

Vegetables: potato, carrot, cauliflower, swede, butternut squash, pumpkin and sweet potato

Fruit: apple, pear and banana

Ready-made baby foods (suitable for four months)

Foods to Avoid

Meat, fish, poultry

Wheat products – bread, pasta, breakfast cereals, flour

Rye, barley, oats

Milk other than breast or formula milk

Yoghurt

Cheese

Eggs

Nuts

Citrus and berry fruits

Honey

Salt

Sugar

Useful Equipment

Small shallow plastic spoons

Plastic bowls

Large absorbent bib

Hand blender, baby mill or sieve for making purées

Two-handled baby cup

Kitchen paper or wipes for clearing up the mess

Keep it clean
- Always wash your hands before you start and between each stage of food preparation
- Wash all the kitchen utensils and equipment extra carefully in very hot water. Scald your baby's spoons, cups and bowls with boiling water just before you use them. You don't need to sterilise them
- Don't keep your baby's leftovers as they will be contaminated with saliva and bacteria will multiply
- You can keep untouched cooked food in the fridge for 24 hours
- Food must be reheated thoroughly to kill all the bacteria in it. Heat until piping hot all the way through then cool before serving lukewarm to your baby
- When defrosting frozen food, make sure that is completely thawed, then heat it stirring well to make sure that it is heated right through
- Never heat milk in a microwave
- When heating food in a microwave, make sure the food is not too hot before serving to your baby. Stir well to avoid hot spots
- Check the use-by date on ready-made food before you give it to your baby

Food Allergy
If you or your family have a history of allergy, such as asthma or eczema, your baby may be at greater risk of developing a food allergy or intolerance. Speak to your doctor or health visitor before introducing solids – it may be wise to delay the introduction of certain foods. To cut the chances of allergy or intolerance you can:
- Breast feed as long as possible
- Avoid giving solids before four months
- Introduce one food at a time, leaving 2–3 days before introducing the next food. If you notice any problem, stop feeding your baby the newest food and speak to your doctor.

Do not give any of the following foods before six months: wheat, oats, rye, barley, eggs, cow's milk, cheese, yoghurt, any dairy food, nuts, sesame seeds, oranges or fish.

If you suspect that your baby is allergic to a particular food, speak to your doctor who will be able to refer you to a specialist. Do not exclude foods from your baby's diet without a proper diagnosis and expert advice. If your baby does develop an allergy, be reassured that many babies grow out of their allergy by the age of five.

NUT ALLERGY

Nuts can cause serious allergies in a few children and peanuts seem to cause the worst reactions. The exact cause is not known but children with nut allergies often have other allergies and other allergy-related conditions such as asthma, hay fever and eczema. A family history of allergy also increases the risk of a child developing a nut allergy. It is recommended that young children under three with a personal or family history of allergy should not be given peanuts in any form. Children with no allergy history can be given peanuts and other nut products after the age of one. Whole nuts and seeds should not be given to children under five because of the risk of choking but they can be used finely ground or as smooth spreads, e.g. peanut butter.

MEAL PLANNER – FOUR MONTHS

WEEK 1	Early morning	Breakfast	Lunch	Tea	Bedtime
Days 1–3	Breast or formula milk	Breast or formula milk	1–2 teaspoons baby rice Breast or formula milk	Breast or formula milk	Breast or formula milk
Day 4	Breast or formula milk	Breast or formula milk	Pear purée (p 43)	Breast or formula milk	Breast or formula milk
Day 5	Breast or formula milk	Breast or formula milk	1–2 teaspoons baby rice Breast or formula milk	Breast or formula milk	Breast or formula milk
Day 6	Breast or formula milk	Breast or formula milk	Pear purée (p 43)	Breast or formula milk	Breast or formula milk
Day 7	Breast or formula milk	Breast or formula milk	1–2 teaspoons baby rice Breast or formula milk	Breast or formula milk	Breast or formula milk

WEEK 2	Early morning	Breakfast	Lunch	Tea	Bedtime
Day 1	Breast or formula milk	Breast or formula milk	Apple cream (p 47) Breast or formula milk	Breast or formula milk	Breast or formula milk
Day 2	Breast or formula milk	Breast or formula milk	Apple purée (p 42) Breast or formula milk	Breast or formula milk	Breast or formula milk
Day 3	Breast or formula milk	Breast or formula milk	Pear purée (p 43) Breast or formula milk	Breast or formula milk	Breast or formula milk
Day 4	Breast or formula milk	Breast or formula milk	Pear purée (p 43) Breast or formula milk	Breast or formula milk	Breast or formula milk
Day 5	Breast or formula milk	Breast or formula milk	Orchard purée (p 45) Breast or formula milk	Breast or formula milk	Breast or formula milk
Day 6	Breast or formula milk	Breast or formula milk	Orchard purée (p 45) Breast or formula milk	Breast or formula milk	Breast or formula milk
Day 7	Breast or formula milk	Breast or formula milk	Orchard purée (p 45) Breast or formula milk	Breast or formula milk	Breast or formula milk

WEEK 3	Early morning	Breakfast	Lunch	Tea	Bedtime
Day 1	Breast or formula milk	Baby rice Breast or formula milk	Perfect potatoes (p 36) Breast or formula milk	Breast or formula milk	Breast or formula milk
Day 2	Breast or formula milk	Apple cream (p 47) Breast or formula milk	Perfect potatoes (p 36) Breast or formula milk	Breast or formula milk	Breast or formula milk
Day 3	Breast or formula milk	Baby rice Breast or formula milk	Perfect potatoes with carrot (p 36) Breast or formula milk	Breast or formula milk	Breast or formula milk
Day 4	Breast or formula milk	Pear purée (p 43) & Baby rice Breast or formula milk	Perfect potatoes with carrot (p 36) Breast or formula milk	Breast or formula milk	Breast or formula milk
Day 5	Breast or formula milk	Baby rice Breast or formula milk	Carrot and swede purée (p 39) Breast or formula milk	Breast or formula milk	Breast or formula milk
Day 6	Breast or formula milk	Banana purée (p 44) Breast or formula milk	Carrot and swede purée (p 39) Breast or formula milk	Breast or formula milk	Breast or formula milk
Day 7	Breast or formula milk	Baby rice Breast or formula milk	Mixed vegetable purée (p 38) Breast or formula milk	Breast or formula milk	Breast or formula milk

WEEK 4	Early morning	Breakfast	Lunch	Tea	Bedtime
Day1	Breast or formula milk	Pear purée (p 43) & Baby rice Breast or formula milk	Perfect potatoes with swede (p 36) Breast or formula milk	Breast or formula milk	Breast or formula milk
Day2	Breast or formula milk	Apple purée (p 42) & Baby rice Breast or formula milk	Perfect potatoes with sweet potatoes (p 36) Breast or formula milk	Breast or formula milk	Breast or formula milk
Day3	Breast or formula milk	Banana purée (p 44) Breast or formula milk	Parsnip and butternut squash purée (p 40) Breast or formula milk	Breast or formula milk	Breast or formula milk
Day 4	Breast or formula milk	Orchard purée (p 45) Breast or formula milk	Vegetable and rice dinner (p 41) Breast or formula milk	Breast or formula milk	Breast or formula milk
Day 5	Breast or formula milk	Apple purée (p 42) & Baby rice Breast orformula milk	Perfect potatoes with swede (p 36) Breast or formula milk	Breast or formula milk	Breast or formula milk
Day 6	Breast or formula milk	Pear and banana purée (p 46) Breast or formula milk	Mixed vegetable purée (p 38) Breast or formula milk	Breast or formula milk	Breast or formula milk
Day 7	Breast or formula milk	Apricot rice (p 48) Breast or formula milk	Carrot and swede purée (p 39) Breast or formula milk	Breast or formula milk	Breast or formula milk

RECIPES
FOR BABIES
FROM FOUR
MONTHS
●●●●

Perfect Potatoes

●●●●

1 large potato (about 125g/4 oz)
Breast or formula milk

Peel and chop the potato. Bring about 125ml (4 fl oz) water to the boil in a small saucepan. Add the potato, cover, turn down the heat and simmer for about 15 minutes until tender. Drain.

Alternatively, scrub the potato, prick and bake in the oven for about 40 minutes or microwave on high power for about 5 minutes.

Mash the cooked flesh with baby milk then purée in a blender or press through a sieve. Add more milk for a thinner consistency.

 MAKES:
4 PORTIONS

 STORAGE: 24 HOURS IN THE FRIDGE;
4 WEEKS IN THE FREEZER

 PREPARATION: 5 MINUTES PLUS
15 MINUTES COOKING TIME

 NUTRITION: GOOD SOURCE OF
COMPLEX CARBOHYDRATES, VITAMIN C

TIP
Parsnips, carrots and butternut squash may be cooked the same way. Adjust the consistency with a little of the cooking liquid or your baby's usual milk.

Potato Partners
Potato provides an ideal base to combine with other vegetables. Use approximately equal quantities of potato and any of the following vegetables:
Carrot
Swede
Parsnip
Pumpkin
Butternut squash
Sweet potato

Mixed Vegetable Purée

● ● ● ●

1 small sweet potato or potato, peeled and chopped
1 small parsnip, peeled and chopped
¹/₂ swede, peeled and chopped

Bring a little water to the boil in a saucepan, add the prepared vegetables, reduce the heat then simmer for about 15 minutes until tender.

Alternatively, steam or microwave the vegetables until tender.

Allow to cool slightly then purée with a hand-held blender or in a food processor or blender until smooth.

You can add a little of the cooking liquid or your baby's usual milk to get a thinner consistency.

Serve lukewarm.

 MAKES:
8–10 PORTIONS

 STORAGE: 24 HOURS IN THE FRIDGE;
4 WEEKS IN THE FREEZER

 PREPARATION: 10 MINUTES PLUS
15 MINUTES COOKING TIME

 NUTRITION: GOOD SOURCE OF COMPLEX CARBOHYDRATES,
VITAMINS A (BETA-CAROTENE) AND C

Carrot and Swede Purée

●●●●

1 carrot, peeled and sliced
¹/₂ swede, peeled and chopped

Bring a little water to the boil in a saucepan, add the carrot and swede, reduce the heat then simmer for about 15 minutes until tender.

Alternatively, steam or microwave the vegetables until tender.

Allow to cool slightly then purée with a hand-held blender or in a food processor or blender until smooth.

You can add a little of the cooking liquid or your baby's usual milk to get a thinner consistency.

Serve lukewarm.

 MAKES:
6 PORTIONS

 STORAGE: 24 HOURS IN THE FRIDGE;
4 WEEKS IN THE FREEZER

 PREPARATION: 10 MINUTES PLUS
15 MINUTES COOKING TIME

 NUTRITION: GOOD SOURCE OF VITAMIN A
(BETA-CAROTENE), POTASSIUM, FIBRE

Parsnip and Butternut Squash Purée

●●●●

1 parsnip, peeled and sliced
1 wedge of butternut squash, peeled and diced

Bring a little water to the boil in a small saucepan. Add the vegetables, reduce the heat, cover and cook for 10 minutes until tender. Drain.

Purée the vegetables with a hand-held blender or in a food processor or blender until smooth. Add a little breast or formula milk for a more runny consistency.

Serve lukewarm.

MAKES:
6 PORTIONS

STORAGE: 24 HOURS IN THE FRIDGE;
4 WEEKS IN THE FREEZER

PREPARATION: 5 MINUTES PLUS
10 MINUTES COOKING TIME

NUTRITION: GOOD SOURCE OF COMPLEX
CARBOHYDRATES, VITAMIN A (BETA-CAROTENE)

Vegetable and Rice Dinner

••••

1 carrot, peeled and chopped
1 parsnip, peeled and chopped
30ml (2 tbsp) baby rice
Breast or formula milk

Bring a little water to the boil in a saucepan, add the vegetables, reduce the heat then simmer for about 15 minutes until tender.

Alternatively, steam or microwave the vegetables until tender.

Allow to cool slightly then purée with a hand-held blender or in a food processor or blender until smooth.

Mix the baby rice with the milk according to the instructions on the packet. Stir into the vegetable purée until well combined.

Serve lukewarm.

 MAKES:
8 PORTIONS

 STORAGE: 24 HOURS IN THE FRIDGE;
4 WEEKS IN THE FREEZER

 PREPARATION: 10 MINUTES PLUS
15 MINUTES COOKING TIME

 NUTRITION: GOOD SOURCE OF COMPLEX CARBOHYDRATES,
VITAMIN A (BETA-CAROTENE), FIBRE

Apple Purée

●●●●

1 eating apple, peeled, cored and sliced

Put the apple in a saucepan with approximately 4 tablespoons of water. Bring to the boil, cover and simmer for 10 minutes. Stir occasionally, checking that the fruit has not caught the bottom of the pan. Alternatively, microwave on high power for 3 minutes.

Blend to a purée with a hand-held blender or in a food processor or blender until smooth, adding a little cooled boiled water if you want a thinner consistency.

 MAKES:
2 PORTIONS

 STORAGE: 24 HOURS IN THE FRIDGE;
4 WEEKS IN THE FREEZER

 PREPARATION: 5 MINUTES PLUS
10 MINUTES COOKING TIME

 NUTRITION: GOOD SOURCE OF
FIBRE, VITAMIN C

Pear Purée

● ● ● ●

1 ripe pear, peeled, cored and sliced

Put the prepared pear in a saucepan with approximately 4 tablespoons of water. Bring to the boil, cover and simmer for 10 minutes. Stir occasionally, checking that the fruit has not caught the bottom of the pan. Alternatively, microwave on high power for 3 minutes.

Blend to a purée with a hand-held blender or in a food processor or blender until smooth, adding a little cooled boiled water if you want a thinner consistency.

 MAKES:
2 PORTIONS

 STORAGE: 24 HOURS IN THE FRIDGE;
4 WEEKS IN THE FREEZER

 PREPARATION: 5 MINUTES PLUS
10 MINUTES COOKING TIME

 NUTRITION: GOOD SOURCE OF
POTASSIUM, VITAMIN C

Banana Purée

●●●●

5-cm (2-inch) piece of very ripe banana
15ml (1 tbsp) breast or formula milk

Mash the banana with a fork to make it very smooth or press through a sieve.

Stir in the milk (or cooled boiled water) to make a runny consistency. Serve straight away.

 MAKES:
1 PORTION

 STORAGE: UNSUITABLE –
USE STRAIGHT AWAY

 PREPARATION:
5 MINUTES

 NUTRITION: GOOD SOURCE OF
CARBOHYDRATE, FIBRE, VITAMIN B6

Orchard Purée
●●●●

1 eating apple, peeled, cored and finely sliced
1 pear, peeled, cored and chopped

Put the apple and pear in a saucepan with approximately
4 tablespoons of water. Bring to the boil, cover and simmer
for 10 minutes. Stir occasionally, checking that the fruit has
not caught the bottom of the pan. Alternatively, microwave
on high power for 4 minutes.

Blend to a purée, adding a little cooled boiled water
if necessary.

 MAKES:
4 PORTIONS

 STORAGE: 24 HOURS IN THE FRIDGE;
4 WEEKS IN THE FREEZER

 PREPARATION: 5 MINUTES PLUS
10 MINUTES COOKING TIME

 NUTRITION: GOOD SOURCE OF
FIBRE, VITAMIN C, POTASSIUM

TIP
Use ripe, naturally sweet fruit.

Pear and Banana Purée

●●●●

1 ripe pear, peeled, cored and chopped
1 ripe banana

Cook the pear in a small pan with 2–3 tablespoons of water.
Simmer gently for about 10 minutes.

Purée the pear with the banana using a blender.

MAKES:
4 PORTIONS

STORAGE: 24 HOURS
IN THE FRIDGE

PREPARATION: 5 MINUTES PLUS
10 MINUTES COOKING TIME

NUTRITION: GOOD SOURCE OF
CARBOHYDRATE, POTASSIUM, FIBRE

TIP
Chose bananas that have light brown speckling. Unripe bananas
are indigestible for a baby's immature digestive system.

Apple Cream

●●●●

1 eating apple, peeled, cored and sliced
60ml (4 tbsp) water
30ml (2 tbsp) baby rice
Breast or formula milk

Cook the apple in the water for about 10 minutes or until soft.

Mix the baby rice with breast or formula milk according to the instructions on the packet.

Purée the cooked apple with the rice.

🕐 **MAKES:**
6 PORTIONS

❄ **STORAGE: 24 HOURS IN THE FRIDGE;**
4 WEEKS IN THE FREEZER

🕐 **PREPARATION: 5 MINUTES PLUS**
10 MINUTES COOKING TIME

☺ **NUTRITION: GOOD SOURCE OF**
VITAMIN C, CARBOHYDRATE, PROTEIN

Apricot Rice

●●●●

1 canned apricot in fruit juice, drained
30ml (2 tbsp) baby rice
Breast or formula milk

Make up the baby rice with milk according to the instructions on the packet.

Purée with the apricot until smooth.

MAKES:
2 PORTIONS

STORAGE: 24 HOURS IN THE FRIDGE,
4 WEEKS IN THE FREEZER

PREPARATION:
5 MINUTES

NUTRITION: GOOD SOURCE OF
VITAMIN A (BETA-CAROTENE)

Polenta Porridge

••••

15ml (1 tbsp) polenta (cornmeal)
45ml (3 tbsp) breast or formula milk

Mix the polenta with the milk.

Cook over a gentle heat for 3–4 minutes until smooth and slightly thickened. Alternatively, cook in a microwave for 2–3 minutes.

Allow to cool and serve lukewarm or at room temperature. Add extra milk for a thinner consistency.

 MAKES:
2 PORTIONS

 STORAGE: 24 HOURS IN THE FRIDGE,
4 WEEKS IN THE FREEZER

 PREPARATION:
5 MINUTES

 NUTRITION: GOOD SOURCE OF
CARBOHYDRATE, IRON, PROTEIN

TIP
Polenta, or cornmeal, is gluten-free so it is suitable for babies under six months. It makes a change from baby rice and provides carbohydrate and small amounts of iron and protein. You can use it to make a smooth porridge, as in this recipe, or use it to thicken vegetable and fruit purées.

Chapter 3
From Five to Six Months

Your baby may now be ready for three solid meals a day and a slightly more adventurous diet.

STRONGER FLAVOURS

Build on the flavours your baby already likes and gradually introduce combinations with new flavours. Aim for one new food every three or four days. You can offer vegetables with stronger flavours, such as broccoli and spinach, and a wider variety of fruit, such as avocado, papaya, mango and melon. It takes time for babies to accept new tastes so don't worry if your baby spits it out. Just try again in a few days.

INTRODUCE PROTEIN

After about five months, you can introduce small amounts of protein foods, such as puréed cooked red lentils or small amounts of well-cooked chicken or turkey breast mixed with vegetables. Try tiny amounts of plain whole milk yoghurt or fromage frais, perhaps mixed with puréed fruit. However, if there is a family history of asthma or eczema it is best to wait until six months before giving dairy foods.

FREEZING BABY FOOD

Cooking food in bulk and then freezing meal-sized portions saves a lot of time. Ice cube trays are ideal for small appetites. Transfer the frozen portions to freezer bags. You can also use small-lidded pots or freezer bags. Remember to include the date on the label. You can keep most home-made baby food in a three-star freezer compartment for up to four weeks. Defrost portions gently, then re-heat it thoroughly, allowing it to cool before feeding to your baby.

SUITABLE FOODS FOR FIVE TO SIX MONTHS

Foods to include:
Serve as purées
- Vegetables: potato, swede, parsnip, turnip, carrot, broccoli, peas, cauliflower, spinach
- Chicken and turkey
- Fruit: apple, pear, banana, apricot, peach, plum, papaya, mango, melon
- White fish e.g. cod, plaice (check for bones)
- Split lentils
- Plain yoghurt
- Ready made baby food (from 4 months)

Foods to avoid
- Salt
- Sugar
- Honey
- Wheat – bread, pasta, breakfast cereals, flour
- Rye, barley, oats
- Milk other than breast or formula milk
- Hard cheese
- Eggs
- Citrus and berry fruits
- Red meat
- Offal
- Pâté
- Mould-ripened soft cheese (e.g. Brie) and blue cheese

Tip
*Andrea McLean (GMTV weather girl): I find it useful to spend
a day cooking huge batches of food for Finlay, steaming apples,
pears and other soft fruit, mashing them up then storing in ice
cube trays in the freezer. I do the same with vegetable mixtures
so I have enough food to feed him for a few weeks.*

WHAT ABOUT COMMERCIAL BABY FOODS?

Although I would not recommend a diet made up only of
commercial baby food, they are certainly convenient when you're
out and about. You can feed your baby straight from the jar or tin
(throw away any leftovers, though) or spoon out the amount your
baby needs and keep the remainder in the fridge.

It's a good idea to keep a few jars or packets in the cupboard as
stand-bys. They are handy to have when you have unexpected
baby visitors or when you have a ravenous baby demanding to be
fed but no time to prepare anything!

Choose baby foods suitable for your baby's age group and,
before you buy, always check the labels for unnecessary
ingredients. Some varieties are as nutritious as home-prepared
meals but others may contain added sugar, salt, artificial additives,
thickeners and fillers (such as maltodextrin and modified starch).

DRINKING FROM A CUP

Babies are ready to start drinking from a cup between four and six
months. A good time to start the change from bottle to cup is when
you introduce your baby to first weaning foods. Your aim should be
to make the changeover from bottle to cup by your baby's first

birthday. This will protect teeth, help to establish good eating patterns and help avoid speech problems. Here are some tips:

• Use a cup as a toy early on
• Use a cup at mealtimes during weaning
• A cup without a lid is the best choice – it encourages your baby to develop a sipping action when drinking. Two handles allow better control. If you're unhappy about spillages, choose a lidded cup where the drink can flow without sucking. Valve feeder cups, any-way-up cups and no-spill cups are to be avoided because they still need to be sucked hard
• Milk and water are the only safe drinks for teeth
• Be patient if your baby has any spills and accidents

WEANING TIMETABLE

Here is a general guide to weaning your baby:

Week 1
Give your baby one or two teaspoons of baby rice midway through one of the milk feeds.

Week 2
Increase the amount of baby rice if your baby wants more. Introduce small tastes of smooth puréed mild vegetables and fruit, perhaps alternating with the rice meals and diluted with a little baby rice

Week 3
If your baby is enjoying solids, offer two meals a day in addition to the milk feeds, perhaps alternating a rice meal and a vegetable or fruit purée meal.

Week 4

Increase the portion sizes if your baby wants more. Continue to introduce new foods (see Suitable Foods For Five To Six Months, p 51).

Week 5

Continue to give your baby's milk feeds and two solid meals a day. Your baby may be ready for a third meal. Be guided by your baby's appetite and preferences.

Week 6

Continue to introduce new foods and flavour combinations. If your baby rejects a food, try again a few days later.

Weeks 7 and 8

Your baby should have established a good routine by this stage. After an early morning milk feed, offer a baby cereal for breakfast plus a milk feed. For lunch, give a vegetable purée plus a drink of cooled boiled water or unsweetened fruit juice (dilute 1 part juice to at least 3 parts water). For tea, offer a vegetable or fruit purée plus a milk feed and a further milk feed at bedtime.

LOOKING AFTER YOUR BABY'S TEETH

- Milk and cooled boiled water are the safest drinks for your baby's teeth
- Avoid squash, fruit drinks, and even 'baby' drinks as they contain sugar and fruit acids, which are harmful for your baby's soft teeth
- Well-diluted fruit juice (1 part juice to at least 2 parts water) is a safer drink but should only be given at mealtimes. Offer in a cup rather than a bottle
- Bottles should only be used for milk or water – sucking sweetened drinks bathes the front teeth in sugar, increasing the chances of decay and erosion
- Encourage your baby to drink from a feeder cup from about six months of age
- Once your baby has finished the milk in a bottle or fallen asleep, remove from the mouth straight away – this prevents pooling of milk around the teeth, which can lead to decay

MEAL PLANNER FIVE TO SIX MONTHS

WEEK 1	Early morning	Breakfast	Lunch	Tea	Bedtime
Day 1	Breast or formula milk	Breast or formula milk Baby cereal	Breast or formula milk Sweet potato and broccoli purée (p 58)	Apple purée (p 42) Breast or formula milk	Breast or formula milk
Day 2	Breast or formula milk	Apple purée (p 42) & Baby rice Breast or formula milk	Spring vegetable medley (p 63)	Mango purée (p 70) Breast or formula milk	Breast or formula milk
Day 3	Breast or formula milk	Banana purée (p 44) Breast or formula milk	Courgette and potato purée (p 62)	Apple and apricot purée (p 67) Breast or formula milk	Breast or formula milk
Day 4	Breast or formula milk	Pear purée (p 43) & Baby rice Breast or formula milk	Vegetable and rice dinner (p 41)	Chicken and vegetable casserole (p 61) or Lentil and vegetable feast (p 64) Breast or formula milk	Breast or formula milk
Day 5	Breast or formula milk	Baby cereal Breast or formula milk	Vegetable medley (p 57)	Plum and pear purée (p 69) Breast or formula milk	Breast or formula milk
Day 6	Breast or formula milk	Apple and apricot purée (p 67) Breast or formula milk	Chicken and vegetable casserole (p 61) or Lentil and vegetable feast (p 64)	Carrot and courgette purée (p 60) Breast or formula milk	Breast or formula milk
Day 7	Breast or formula milk	Banana purée (p 44) Breast or formula milk	Popeye purée (p 59)	Avocado purée (p 70) Breast or formula milk	Breast or formula milk

RECIPES
FOR BABIES
FROM FIVE
MONTHS
●●●●●

Vegetable Medley

●●●●●

1 potato peeled and chopped
1 carrot, peeled and chopped
1 handful frozen peas

Bring a little water to the boil in a small saucepan.
Add the potato and carrot, cover and simmer for about
8 minutes. Add the frozen peas and continue cooking
for 4 minutes.

Purée the vegetables with about 1 tablespoon of
the cooking liquid in a mouli or with a hand blender
or in a liquidiser. Add a little extra cooking liquid for
a thinner consistency.

Serve lukewarm.

 MAKES:
4 PORTIONS

 STORAGE: 24 HOURS IN THE FRIDGE;
4 WEEKS IN THE FREEZER

 PREPARATION: 10 MINUTES PLUS
12 MINUTES COOKING TIME

 NUTRITION: GOOD SOURCE OF VITAMINS A
(BETA-CAROTENE) AND C COMPLEX CARBOHYDRATES

Sweet Potato and Broccoli Purée

●●●●●

1 small sweet potato, peeled and chopped
4 sprigs broccoli
15ml (1 tbsp) breast or formula milk

Bring a little water to the boil in a small saucepan. Add the sweet potato and broccoli. Cover, reduce the heat and simmer for 12–15 minutes or until they are tender. Alternatively, cook the vegetables in the microwave.

Drain then purée with the milk with a hand-held blender or in a food processor or blender until smooth.

Serve lukewarm.

 MAKES:
8 PORTIONS

 STORAGE: 24 HOURS IN THE FRIDGE;
4 WEEKS IN THE FREEZER

 PREPARATION: 5 MINUTES PLUS
15 MINUTES COOKING TIME

 NUTRITION: GOOD SOURCE OF VITAMINS A
(BETA-CAROTENE) AND C, FOLIC ACID

TIP
You may substitute potato for the sweet potato.

Popeye Purée

●●●●●

1 potato (approx. 125g (4 oz)), peeled and chopped
85g (3 oz) baby spinach, washed
15ml (1 tbsp) breast or formula milk

Cook the potato in a little fast-boiling water for 10 minutes. Add the spinach and continue cooking for a further 5 minutes. Drain, reserving the cooking liquid.

Purée the vegetables with the milk and 1 tablespoon (15 ml) of the cooking liquid with a hand-held blender or in a food processor or blender until smooth.

Serve lukewarm.

 MAKES:
6 PORTIONS

 STORAGE: 24 HOURS IN THE FRIDGE;
4 WEEKS IN THE FREEZER

 PREPARATION: 5 MINUTES PLUS
15 MINUTES COOKING TIME

 NUTRITION: GOOD SOURCE OF VITAMINS A
(BETA-CAROTENE) AND C, IRON

TIP
Mixing stronger tasting vegetables such as spinach with potato is a good way to introduce them to your baby.

Carrot and Courgette Purée

•••••

1 carrot, peeled and sliced
1 courgette, sliced

Bring a little water to the boil in a saucepan, add the carrot, reduce the heat, cover and simmer for about 5 minutes.

Add the courgette and continue cooking for a further 5 minutes. Drain.

Blend to a purée with a hand-held blender or in a food processor or blender until smooth, adding a little cooking water to thin if necessary.

Serve lukewarm.

 MAKES:
4 PORTIONS

 STORAGE: 24 HOURS IN THE FRIDGE;
4 WEEKS IN THE FREEZER

 PREPARATION: 5 MINUTES PLUS
10 MINUTES COOKING TIME

 NUTRITION: GOOD SOURCE OF POTASSIUM
VITAMIN A (BETA-CAROTENE), FIBRE

Chicken and Vegetable Casserole

●●●●●

1 medium potato, peeled and diced
60g (2 oz) skinless, boneless chicken breast, diced
1 small carrot, peeled and sliced
2 sprigs of cauliflower
150ml (5 fl oz) water or breast or formula milk

Place the vegetables and chicken in a saucepan with the water or milk. Bring to the boil, cover, reduce the heat and simmer for 15 minutes until the vegetables and chicken are tender.

Purée with a hand-held blender or in a food processor or blender until smooth.

You can add a little extra milk or water to get a thinner consistency.

Serve lukewarm.

 MAKES:
4 PORTIONS

 STORAGE: 24 HOURS IN THE FRIDGE;
4 WEEKS IN THE FREEZER

 PREPARATION: 10 MINUTES PLUS
15 MINUTES COOKING TIME

 NUTRITION: GOOD SOURCE OF PROTEIN
VITAMIN A (BETA-CAROTENE), B VITAMINS

Courgette and Potato Purée

●●●●●

1 potato, peeled and chopped
1 courgette, trimmed and sliced

Bring a little water to the boil in a small saucepan.
Add the potato, reduce the heat, cover and cook for
10 minutes.

Add the courgette and continue cooking for a further 4–5 minutes,
until tender. Drain, reserving the cooking liquid.

Purée the vegetables with a hand-held blender or in a food
processor or blender until smooth. Add a little of the reserved
cooking liquid for a more runny consistency.

Serve lukewarm.

 MAKES:
4 PORTIONS

 STORAGE: 24 HOURS IN THE FRIDGE;
4 WEEKS IN THE FREEZER

 PREPARATION: 5 MINUTES PLUS
15 MINUTES COOKING TIME

 NUTRITION: GOOD SOURCE OF
VITAMIN C, COMPLEX CARBOHYDRATES

Spring Vegetable Medley
● ● ● ● ●

3 florets of broccoli
3 florets of cauliflower
Handful of peas

Bring a little water to the boil in a small saucepan. Add the broccoli and cauliflower, reduce the heat, cover and cook for 5 minutes.

Add the peas and continue cooking for a further 4–5 minutes, until tender. Drain, reserving the cooking liquid.

Purée the vegetables with a hand-held blender or in a food processor or blender until smooth. Add a little of the reserved cooking liquid for a more runny consistency.

Serve lukewarm.

MAKES:
6 PORTIONS

STORAGE: 24 HOURS IN THE FRIDGE;
4 WEEKS IN THE FREEZER

PREPARATION: 5 MINUTES PLUS
15 MINUTES COOKING TIME

NUTRITION: GOOD SOURCE OF VITAMINS A
(BETA-CAROTENE) AND C, IRON

TIP
This colourful green purée is packed with vitamin C.

Lentil and Vegetable Feast

●●●●●

30ml (2 tbsp) red lentils
250ml (8 fl oz) water
1 carrot, peeled and sliced
1 potato, peeled and chopped
½ swede, peeled and chopped

Put the lentils, water and vegetables in a saucepan. Bring to the boil, cover and simmer for about 30 minutes or until the lentils are quite mushy. Top up with a little more water during cooking, if necessary.

Purée with a hand-held blender or in a food processor or blender until smooth.

Serve lukewarm.

TIP

The lentil purée thickens slightly as it cools so you may need to add a little breast or formula milk before serving.

MAKES:
4 PORTIONS

STORAGE: 24 HOURS IN THE FRIDGE;
4 WEEKS IN THE FREEZER

PREPARATION: 5 MINUTES PLUS
30 MINUTES COOKING TIME

NUTRITION: GOOD SOURCE OF PROTEIN
IRON, B VITAMINS, VITAMIN A (BETA-CAROTENE)

Three Fruits Purée

•••••

1 eating apple, peeled, cored and sliced
1 ripe pear, peeled, cored and chopped
1 ripe plum, stoned and quartered
60ml (4 tbsp) water

Place the prepared fruit in a saucepan with the water. Bring to the boil, reduce the heat, cover and simmer gently for 10 minutes until the fruit is soft.

Purée the fruit in a hand-held blender or in a food processor or blender until smooth.

Allow the mixture to cool before serving.

MAKES:
5 PORTIONS

STORAGE: 24 HOURS IN THE FRIDGE;
3 MONTHS IN THE FREEZER

PREPARATION: 10 MINUTES PLUS
10 MINUTES COOKING TIME

NUTRITION: GOOD SOURCE OF
FIBRE, POTASSIUM

Mango and Banana Purée

●●●●●

½ ripe mango
½ ripe banana, peeled

Slice through the mango either side of the stone.
Peel, then cut the flesh into cubes.

Purée the mango and banana with a hand-held blender or in a
food processor or blender until smooth.

MAKES:
4 PORTIONS

STORAGE: 24 HOURS IN THE FRIDGE;
4 WEEKS IN THE FREEZER

PREPARATION: 10 MINUTES PLUS
10 MINUTES COOKING TIME

NUTRITION: GOOD SOURCE OF
BETA-CAROTENE, POTASSIUM, VITAMIN C

Apple and Apricot Purée

•••••

1 eating apple, peeled and sliced
2 ripe apricots (or use 4 dried ready-to-eat apricots)
60ml (4 tbsp) water

Place the apple and apricots in a saucepan with the water.

Bring to the boil, reduce the heat, cover and simmer for 10 minutes, checking from time to time that the fruit hasn't caught the bottom of the pan.

Purée the fruit with a hand-held blender or in a food processor or blender until smooth. Add a little extra boiled water if a thinner consistency is needed.

Allow the mixture to cool before serving.

 MAKES:
3–4 PORTIONS

 STORAGE: 24 HOURS IN THE FRIDGE;
4 WEEKS IN THE FREEZER

 PREPARATION: 5 MINUTES PLUS
10 MINUTES COOKING TIME

 NUTRITION: GOOD SOURCE OF
BETA-CAROTENE, POTASSIUM, FIBRE

Peach Purée

●●●●●

1 ripe peach
15ml (1 tbsp) apple juice
15ml (1 tbsp) water

Peel the peach. If the skin doesn't come away easily, place the peach in a bowl of boiling water and leave for one minute. Rinse under cold water. The skin should then come away easily.

Halve the peach, remove the stone, and then slice the flesh. Place in a saucepan with the apple juice and water. Bring to the boil, reduce the heat, cover and simmer gently for 10 minutes until the fruit is soft.

Purée the fruit with a hand-held blender or in a food processor or blender until smooth.

Allow the mixture to cool before serving.

 MAKES:
2 PORTIONS

 STORAGE: 24 HOURS IN THE FRIDGE;
4 WEEKS IN THE FREEZER

 PREPARATION: 5 MINUTES PLUS
10 MINUTES COOKING TIME

 NUTRITION: GOOD SOURCE OF
POTASSIUM, VITAMIN C

TIP
You can make this purée with a nectarine instead of a peach.

Plum and Pear Purée

●●●●●

1 ripe plum, quartered, stone removed
1 pear, peeled, cored and chopped
30ml (2 tbsp) water

Place the prepared fruit in a saucepan with the water. Bring to the boil, reduce the heat, cover and simmer gently for 10 minutes until the fruit is soft.

Purée the fruit with a hand-held blender or in a food processor or blender until smooth.

Allow the mixture to cool before serving.

MAKES:
3 PORTIONS

STORAGE: 24 HOURS IN THE FRIDGE;
4 WEEKS IN THE FREEZER

PREPARATION: 5 MINUTES PLUS
10 MINUTES COOKING TIME

NUTRITION: GOOD SOURCE OF
BETA-CAROTENE, POTASSIUM, FIBRE

No-cook Meals
●●●●●

Fresh fruit purées are packed with vitamins and make ideal convenience meals for babies. Choose ripe fruit and serve one portion straight away.

Banana

Peel and mash half a banana with a fork. For babies under five months, sieve the banana to get an ultra smooth purée. Mix in 1–2 tablespoons of breast or formula milk to thin down the consistency. Serve straight away as banana quickly turns brown. Do not freeze.

Melon

Halve or quarter a melon and discard the seeds. Scoop out the flesh and whiz with a hand blender or in a food processor. Serve one portion immediately and freeze the remainder in sections of an ice cube tray. Try Galia, Charentais and Cantaloupe melons – they have the sweetest flesh.

Papaya

Halve a papaya and scoop out the seeds. Purée or mash the flesh until smooth. Serve one portion immediately and freeze the remainder in sections of an ice cube tray.

Avocado

Cut a small ripe avocado in half, remove the stone and scoop out the flesh. Mash or purée the flesh with a little breast or formula milk. Serve immediately. Do not freeze.

Mango

Slice through a very ripe mango either side of the stone. Peel, then cut the flesh into cubes. Purée or mash the flesh until smooth.

TIP

Mangos are naturally very sweet and easy to digest. They are an excellent source of beta-carotene.

Chapter 4
From Six to Nine Months

You'll notice many changes in your baby as he or she continues to grow and develop quickly. Your baby may be able to sit up unaided for a while and will progress from a bouncy chair to a high chair. Your baby will be able to hold a spoon and eat finger foods.

VARIETY

You can now offer a much wider variety of foods to your baby. Most fruit and vegetables are suitable but you may need to sieve the pips from berry fruit. You can start using full fat cow's milk on cereals and in home-made dishes (but not as the main drink). Wheat and wheat-based foods such as pasta, bread and cereals can now be given, although, if there is a family history of allergy to particular foods, ask your health visitor for advice. Lean meat, fish, poultry, lentils and beans can be included, but take care to remove any hidden bones in fish. Mash beans and lentils well.

THICKER, LUMPIER TEXTURES

At six months, your baby's food should still be smooth, but you can make the purées a little thicker and lumpier. From about seven months, you can start giving your baby mashed or finely minced food. This is important as it encourages your baby to chew – even without teeth.

SUITABLE FOODS FOR SIX TO NINE MONTHS

Foods to include:
- Wheat-based foods such as pasta, bread and breadsticks
- Breakfast cereals, with no or little added sugar, e.g. Weetabix, Instant porridge
- Cow's milk on cereals or as part of a dish
- Yoghurt and fromage frais
- Hard cheese
- Lean red meat, mild fish, poultry
- Lentils and beans (well cooked)
- All vegetables
- All fruit (including citrus and berry fruit)
- Egg yolk (well cooked and mashed)
- Dried fruit (small portions)

Foods to avoid:
- Whole or chopped nuts
- Offal (liver, kidney)
- Egg white
- Salty food
- Sugary food
- Honey
- Nuts
- Mould-ripened soft cheese (e.g. Brie) and blue cheese

FINGER FOODS

Your baby may enjoy holding and gnawing finger foods. Finger
foods encourage your baby to chew, bite and self-feed as well as
develop speech muscles. Try chunks of peeled apple or pear, lightly
cooked broccoli spears, cubes of cheese or cooked pasta shapes.
Harder finger foods help comfort sore gums when your baby is
teething. Try fingers of toast, breadsticks or hard baked crusts.

MILK AND DRINKS

Milk is still an important part of your baby's diet – he or she should be getting about 600 ml (1 pint) a day. Breast or formula or follow-on milk should be his or her main drink for the first year, but you can use full-fat cow's milk on cereal or in cooked dishes.

Once your baby is on three solid meals a day, it's best to stop giving milk at mealtimes as it may reduce your baby's appetite for food. Instead, offer a drink of boiled cooled water or well diluted unsweetened fruit juice (1 part juice with at least 2 parts water). Your baby may want a milk feed mid-morning and afternoon.

TIP
Dr Hilary Jones: Introduce lots of different flavours and textures and make food fun for your children. I got my kids to eat broccoli by calling them 'little trees'!

IRON

Your baby's iron stores from birth start to run out around six months. After this it is important that your baby's diet supplies iron to meet his or her needs. Iron deficiency can lead to anaemia, which can delay your baby's growth and development. Include iron-rich foods in your baby's diet (see below). Vitamin C helps the body absorb iron so give your baby vitamin C-rich foods, such as oranges, kiwi fruit, green vegetables and tomatoes, at the same time.
• Iron-rich foods from 6 months
• Green leafy vegetables – broccoli, spinach, green cabbage, curly kale
• Dried apricot or prune purée
• Lentils and beans

- Lean red meat
- Whole grains e.g. wholemeal bread, oat-based cereals
- Iron-fortified baby cereals
- Egg yolk

Tip
Give your baby a spoon to hold at mealtimes and encourage her to try and feed herself. It will be messy so arm yourself with plenty of wipes!

SHOULD I GIVE VITAMIN DROPS?

Most breast-fed babies under six months do not need supplements since breast milk is perfectly matched to young babies' needs. After six months it is recommended that breast-fed babies should be given vitamin drops containing vitamins A, C and D. It's not necessary to give them to formula-fed babies provided they drink at least 500ml (about 1 pint) a day, since all formula milk (including follow-on) is fortified with vitamins.

You can get vitamin drops specially formulated for babies and young children from child health clinics. They are less expensive than commercial brands or may even be free to some parents. Alternatively, you can buy them from chemists and supermarkets.

Tip
Make sure you don't leave your baby unattended while eating because of the possibility of choking
Your baby may see meal times as a game and this may include playing with or throwing food. Try to ignore this as long as she is eating as well as playing. Make it easier on yourself by surrounding the high chair with a plastic mat or newspaper.

MEAL PLANNER SIX TO NINE MONTHS

WEEK 1	DAY 1
Early morning	Breast or formula milk
Breakfast+	Baby cereal with pear purée
Mid-morning	Breast or formula milk
Lunch	Cod with mashed potato (p 85)
Mid-afternoon	Breast or formula milk
Tea+	Toast fingers; Baby yoghurt
Bedtime	Breast or formula milk

WEEK 1	DAY 2
Early morning	Breast or formula milk
Breakfast+	Instant porridge*
Mid-morning	Breast or formula milk
Lunch	Cheesy lentil savoury (p 84)
Mid-afternoon	Breast or formula milk
Tea+	Creamy pasta and tomato (p 94); Fruity custard (p 97)
Bedtime	Breast or formula milk

WEEK 1	DAY 3
Early morning	Breast or formula milk
Breakfast+	Baby cereal with mashed banana
Mid-morning	Breast or formula milk
Lunch	Chicken and vegetable dinner (p 82)
Mid-afternoon	Breast or formula milk
Tea+	Potato and broccoli bake (p 90); Mango fool (p 98)
Bedtime	Breast or formula milk

WEEK 1	DAY 4
Early morning	Breast or formula milk
Breakfast+	Whole-wheat bisk**
Mid-morning	Breast or formula milk
Lunch	Mediterranean pasta (p 88)
Mid-afternoon	Breast or formula milk
Tea+	Minestrone soup (p 79); toast fingers; Melon, kiwi fruit and banana purée (p 95)
Bedtime	Breast or formula milk

WEEK 1	DAY 5
Early morning	Breast or formula milk
Breakfast+	Baby cereal with Apple purée (p 42)
Mid-morning	Breast or formula milk
Lunch	Tuna and broccoli pie (p 89)
Mid-afternoon	Breast or formula milk
Tea+	Cod with mashed potato (p 85); Apple and raspberry purée (p 96)
Bedtime	Breast or formula milk

WEEK 1	DAY 6
Early morning	Breast or formula milk
Breakfast+	Instant porridge*
Mid-morning	Breast or formula milk
Lunch	Cauliflower and broccoli cheese (p 83)
Mid-afternoon	Breast or formula milk
Tea+	Fish in cheese sauce (p 86); Mango fool (p 98)
Bedtime	Breast or formula milk

WEEK 1	DAY 7
Early morning	Breast or formula milk
Breakfast+	Baby cereal with mashed banana
Mid-morning	Breast or formula milk
Lunch	Vegetable risotto (p 80)
Mid-afternoon	Breast or formula milk
Tea+	Cheesy lentil savoury (p 84); Orchard fruit pudding (p 101)
Bedtime	Breast or formula milk

+ With a drink of cooled boiled water or well diluted fruit juice
   (1 part juice with at least 2 parts water)
* Ready Brek or a similar oat cereal
** Weetabix or a similar wheat cereal with no added sugar

RECIPES
FOR BABIES
FROM SIX
MONTHS
●●●●●●

Minestrone Soup

●●●●●●

15ml (1 tbsp) olive oil
1 small onion, chopped
1 carrot, peeled and chopped
Handful of green beans
200ml (¹/₃ pint) vegetable stock (see page 21)
90ml (6 tbsp) passata (smooth sieved tomatoes)
90ml (4 tbsp) tinned haricot beans, drained
60g (2 oz) small pasta shapes

Heat the olive oil in a saucepan. Add the onion and carrot and cook over a medium heat for 7–8 minutes stirring occasionally until the vegetables have softened.

Add the green beans, vegetable stock and passata then bring to the boil.

Reduce the heat, cover and continue cooking for 10 minutes until the vegetables are tender.

Add the beans and pasta and continue cooking for a further 5–10 minutes until the pasta is cooked.

Purée or mash the soup, depending on the age of your baby.

 MAKES:
6 PORTIONS

 STORAGE: 24 HOURS IN THE FRIDGE;
4 WEEKS IN THE FREEZER

 PREPARATION: 10 MINUTES PLUS
25 MINUTES COOKING TIME

 NUTRITION: GOOD SOURCE OF: VITAMINS A (BETA-CAROTENE) AND C,
PROTEIN, COMPLEX CARBOHYDRATES, FIBRE, IRON

Vegetable Risotto

●●●●●●

15ml (1 tbsp) olive oil
1 small onion, finely chopped
1/2 red or yellow pepper, chopped
1 courgette, trimmed and finely sliced
85g (3 oz) rice
350ml (12 fl oz) no-salt vegetable stock
Handful of frozen peas

Heat the oil in a saucepan. Add the onion and peppers and cook for 5 minutes until softened.

Add the courgette and continue cooking for a further 2 minutes.

Add the rice and stir over the heat for a minute or two until the grains have become translucent.

Add the stock and bring to the boil. Turn down the heat and simmer for 15 minutes, stirring from time to time. Add a little extra liquid if necessary.

Add the peas and simmer for a further 5 minutes until the rice and vegetables are tender.

Purée the risotto for younger babies.

MAKES:
8 PORTIONS

STORAGE: 24 HOURS IN THE FRIDGE;
4 WEEKS IN THE FREEZER

PREPARATION: 10 MINUTES PLUS
25–30 MINUTES COOKING TIME

NUTRITION: GOOD SOURCE OF VITAMIN C,
COMPLEX CARBOHYDRATES, FIBRE

Chicken and Vegetable Dinner

●●●●●●

1 small chicken breast (approx. 125g/4 oz),
cut into strips
1 potato, peeled and chopped
2 spears of broccoli
Handful of frozen peas
150ml (¼ pint) vegetable stock (see page 21)
or breast or formula milk

Put the chicken, potatoes and broccoli into a saucepan with the vegetable stock or milk. Bring to the boil, reduce the heat, cover and simmer for 10 minutes.

Add the frozen peas and continue to cook for a further 5 minutes.

Purée the mixture with a hand-held blender or in a food processor or blender until fairly smooth.

Serve lukewarm.

 MAKES:
6 PORTIONS

 STORAGE: 24 HOURS IN THE FRIDGE;
4 WEEKS IN THE FREEZER

 PREPARATION: 5 MINUTES PLUS
15 MINUTES COOKING TIME

 NUTRITION: GOOD SOURCE OF
PROTEIN, VITAMIN C, COMPLEX CARBOHYDRATES, B VITAMINS

Cauliflower and Broccoli Cheese

● ● ● ● ● ●

3 florets cauliflower
3 spears broccoli
15g (½ oz) butter or margarine
15ml (1 tbsp) plain flour
125ml (4 fl oz) full-fat milk
30g (1 oz) Cheddar cheese, grated

Bring a little water to the boil in a small saucepan. Add the cauliflower and broccoli. Cover, reduce the heat and simmer for 10 minutes or until they are tender. Drain.

Meanwhile, melt the butter or margarine in a small saucepan, stir in the flour and slowly add the milk, stirring continuously until the sauce thickens. Turn down the heat and simmer for a minute.

Remove the saucepan from the heat and stir in the grated cheese.

Stir in the cooked vegetables then mash together with a fork or purée until fairly smooth, adding a little extra milk if needed.

Serve lukewarm.

 MAKES:
6 PORTIONS

 STORAGE: 24 HOURS IN THE FRIDGE;
4 WEEKS IN THE FREEZER

 PREPARATION: 10 MINUTES PLUS
10 MINUTES COOKING TIME

 NUTRITION: GOOD SOURCE OF
PROTEIN, VITAMIN C, CALCIUM

Cheesy Lentil Savoury

●●●●●●

30ml (2 tbsp) red lentils
250ml (8 fl oz) water
1 carrot, peeled and sliced
1 small onion, finely chopped
30ml (2 tbsp) Cheddar cheese, grated

Put the lentils, water and vegetables in a saucepan. Bring to the boil, cover and simmer for about 30 minutes or until the lentils are quite mushy. Top up with a little more water during cooking, if necessary.

Stir in the grated cheese. Purée or mash, adding a little milk if you want a thinner consistency. Serve lukewarm.

 MAKES:
2–4 PORTIONS

 STORAGE: 24 HOURS IN THE FRIDGE;
4 WEEKS IN THE FREEZER

 PREPARATION: 10 MINUTES PLUS
30 MINUTES COOKING TIME

 NUTRITION: GOOD SOURCE OF PROTEIN
IRON, FIBRE, VITAMIN A (BETA-CAROTENE)

TIP
Lentils are so good for babies. They are packed with protein and iron, easy to cook and babies love their mealy texture. This was one of Rosie's favourite teatime dishes for many months.

Cod with Mashed Potato

●●●●●●

125g (4 oz) cod fillet
Bay leaf
150ml (¼ pint) full-fat milk
1 large potato, peeled and chopped
½ leek, trimmed and sliced

Put the fish and bay leaf in a small saucepan. Pour over the milk.
Bring to the boil, reduce the heat, part cover the pan and simmer
for about 10 minutes until the fish is cooked.

Remove the fish from the milk using a slotted spoon, flake and roughly
mash with a fork, carefully removing any bones. Reserve the milk.

Meanwhile, cook the potato and leek in a little boiling water for
about 10 minutes or until the vegetables are tender. Drain.

Mash the potato and leek with some of the reserved milk to make a
smooth mixture.

Stir in the flaked fish. Serve lukewarm.

MAKES:
6 PORTIONS

STORAGE: 24 HOURS IN THE FRIDGE;
4 WEEKS IN THE FREEZER

PREPARATION: 10 MINUTES PLUS
10 MINUTES COOKING TIME

NUTRITION: GOOD SOURCE OF PROTEIN
COMPLEX CARBOHYDRATES, B VITAMINS

TIP
*It is fine to use cow's milk in cooking. Breast or formula milk should
continue to be your baby's main drink for the first year.*

Fish in Cheese Sauce

●●●●●●

**125g (4 oz) white fish fillet
(e.g. cod, plaice, haddock, coley)
45ml (3 tbsp) full-fat milk
15g (½ oz) butter or margarine
15ml (1 tbsp) plain flour
125ml (4 fl oz) full-fat milk
30g (1 oz) Cheddar cheese, grated**

Place the fish in a small saucepan and pour over the milk. Bring to the boil, reduce the heat, part cover the pan and simmer for about 10 minutes until the fish is cooked.

Remove the fish from the milk using a slotted spoon, flake and roughly mash with a fork, carefully removing any bones.

Meanwhile, melt the butter or margarine in a small saucepan, stir in the flour and slowly add the milk, stirring continuously until the sauce thickens. Turn down the heat and simmer for a minute.

Remove the saucepan from the heat and stir in the grated cheese.

Stir in the fish, then mash together with a fork, adding a little extra milk if needed.

Serve lukewarm with mashed potatoes and a green vegetable.

MAKES:
6 PORTIONS

STORAGE: 24 HOURS IN THE FRIDGE;
4 WEEKS IN THE FREEZER

PREPARATION: 10 MINUTES PLUS
10 MINUTES COOKING TIME

NUTRITION: GOOD SOURCE OF
PROTEIN, B VITAMINS, CALCIUM

Mediterranean Pasta

●●●●●●●

30g (1 oz) mini pasta shapes
125ml (4 fl oz) vegetable stock (see page 21) or water
30ml (2 tbsp) tinned chopped tomatoes
½ onion, finely chopped
1 courgette, trimmed and sliced
½ red pepper, chopped
Pinch of dried basil

Place the pasta, stock or water, vegetables and basil in a saucepan. Bring to the boil, reduce the heat, part cover the pan and simmer for 10 minutes or until the pasta and vegetables are soft.

Mash with a fork or purée until fairly smooth.

Serve lukewarm.

 MAKES:
6 PORTIONS

 STORAGE: 24 HOURS IN THE FRIDGE;
4 WEEKS IN THE FREEZER

 PREPARATION: 10 MINUTES PLUS
10 MINUTES COOKING TIME

 NUTRITION: GOOD SOURCE OF VITAMIN C,
COMPLEX CARBOHYDRATES, POTASSIUM

Tuna and Broccoli Pie

●●●●●●

1 medium potato, peeled and chopped
3 spears of broccoli
15g (½ oz) butter or margarine
15ml (1 tbsp) plain flour
125ml (4 fl oz) full-fat milk
1 tin (100g) tuna (in water), drained and flaked

Bring a little water to the boil in a saucepan, add the potato and
broccoli, reduce the heat, cover and simmer for about 10 minutes
or until tender. Drain and roughly mash.

Meanwhile, melt the butter or margarine in a small saucepan, stir
in the flour and slowly add the milk, stirring continuously until the
sauce thickens. Turn down the heat and simmer for a minute.

Stir in the mashed vegetables and tuna, transfer to an ovenproof
dish and bake in the oven (190°C/375°F/Gas mark 5) for 15
minutes. Alternatively, cook in the microwave for 3 minutes.

Serve lukewarm.

 MAKES:
6 PORTIONS

 STORAGE: 24 HOURS IN THE FRIDGE;
4 WEEKS IN THE FREEZER

 PREPARATION: 10 MINUTES PLUS
10 MINUTES COOKING TIME

 NUTRITION: GOOD SOURCE OF PROTEIN,
VITAMIN C, COMPLEX CARBOHYDRATES

Potato and Broccoli Bake

••••••

1 potato, peeled and chopped
2 spears of broccoli
15g (^{1}/$_2$ oz) butter or margarine
15ml (1 tbsp) plain flour
125ml (4 fl oz) full-fat milk
45g (1^1/$_2$ oz) Cheddar cheese, grated

Bring a little water to the boil in a small saucepan. Add the potato and broccoli, bring to the boil, reduce the heat, cover and simmer for about 10 minutes until the vegetables are tender. Drain. Roughly chop or mash.

Meanwhile, melt the butter or margarine in a small saucepan, stir in the flour and slowly add the milk, stirring continuously until the sauce thickens. Turn down the heat and simmer for a minute.

Remove the saucepan from the heat and stir in half of the grated cheese.

Add the potatoes and broccoli. Transfer to an ovenproof dish and sprinkle with the remaining grated cheese. Place under a hot grill for a few minutes until bubbling.

Serve lukewarm.

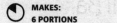

MAKES:
6 PORTIONS

STORAGE: 24 HOURS IN THE FRIDGE;
4 WEEKS IN THE FREEZER

PREPARATION: 10 MINUTES PLUS
10 MINUTES COOKING TIME

NUTRITION: GOOD SOURCE OF VITAMIN C,
COMPLEX CARBOHYDRATES, PROTEIN

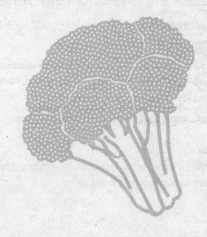

Vegetable Medley

●●●●●●●

1 potato, peeled and chopped
Wedge of green cabbage, chopped
3 spears of broccoli
Handful of peas

Bring a little water to the boil in a saucepan, add the potato, cabbage and broccoli, reduce the heat, cover and simmer for about 5 minutes. Add the peas and continue cooking for a further 5 minutes. Drain.

Mash or blend to a purée with a hand-held blender or in a food processor or blender until fairly smooth.

Serve lukewarm.

 MAKES:
6 PORTIONS

 STORAGE: 24 HOURS IN THE FRIDGE;
4 WEEKS IN THE FREEZER

 PREPARATION: 5 MINUTES PLUS
10 MINUTES COOKING TIME

 NUTRITION: GOOD SOURCE OF VITAMIN C,
COMPLEX CARBOHYDRATES, IRON, FOLIC ACID

TIP
This is a good recipe for introducing stronger tasting vegetables such as cabbage and broccoli.

Cheesy Baked Potatoes
••••••

1 potato
15ml (1 tbsp) plain yoghurt or Greek yoghurt
15ml (1 tbsp) Cheddar cheese, grated
Dot of butter or margarine

Wash the potato, prick with a fork and bake in the oven (200°C/400°F/Gas mark 6) for about 40 minutes.

Remove from the oven, cut in half and scoop out the potato flesh. Mash the flesh with the yoghurt, cheese and butter or margarine.

Pile the mixture back into the potato shells and return to the oven for a further 10 minutes to heat through.

Serve lukewarm, discarding the potato skins if you wish.

MAKES:
2 PORTIONS

STORAGE: 24 HOURS IN THE FRIDGE;
4 WEEKS IN THE FREEZER

PREPARATION: 5 MINUTES PLUS
50 MINUTES COOKING TIME

NUTRITION: GOOD SOURCE OF COMPLEX
CARBOHYDRATES, PROTEIN, CALCIUM

TIP
Bake several potatoes at the same time. Serve to the
rest of your family or freeze for later.

Creamy Pasta and Tomato

●●●●●●

30g (1 oz) mini pasta shapes
15g (¹/₂ oz) butter or margarine
2 tomatoes, skinned, deseeded and chopped
15ml (1 tbsp) plain flour
125ml (4 fl oz) full-fat milk

Cook the pasta in boiling water according to the instructions on the packet. Drain.

Melt the butter or margarine, add the tomatoes and cook for 2 minutes. Stir in the flour and slowly add the milk, stirring continuously until the sauce thickens. Turn down the heat and simmer for a minute.

Stir in the cooked pasta.

Mash or blend to a purée with a hand-held blender or in a food processor or blender until fairly smooth.

Serve lukewarm with an extra vegetable.

 MAKES:
4 PORTIONS

 STORAGE: 24 HOURS IN THE FRIDGE;
4 WEEKS IN THE FREEZER

 PREPARATION: 10 MINUTES PLUS
10 MINUTES COOKING TIME

 NUTRITION: GOOD SOURCE OF COMPLEX
CARBOHYDRATES, PROTEIN, VITAMIN C

TIP
You can serve this dish as it is for older babies and children.

Melon, Kiwi Fruit and Banana Purée

●●●●●●

1 kiwi fruit, peeled and quartered
½ cantaloupe or galia melon,
peeled and roughly chopped
1 small banana, peeled

Purée the fruit in a hand-held blender or in a food processor until smooth.

Add a little baby rice if you need a thicker consistency.

 MAKES:
6 PORTIONS

 STORAGE: 24 HOURS IN THE FRIDGE;
4 WEEKS IN THE FREEZER

 PREPARATION:
10 MINUTES

☺ **NUTRITION: GOOD SOURCE OF VITAMINS A**
(BETA-CAROTENE) AND C, CARBOHYDRATE, POTASSIUM

Apple and Raspberry Purée

● ● ● ● ● ●

1 eating apple, peeled, cored and sliced
15ml (1 tbsp) apple juice
45ml (3 tbsp) water
60 g (2 oz) fresh or frozen raspberries

Put the apple, apple juice and water in a small saucepan. Bring to the boil and simmer gently for 5 minutes.

Add the raspberries and cook for a further 3 minutes, stirring from time to time to prevent the fruit sticking to the bottom.

Push the mixture through a sieve to remove the pips.

Allow to cool before serving.

 MAKES:
3–4 PORTIONS

 STORAGE: 24 HOURS IN THE FRIDGE;
4 WEEKS IN THE FREEZER

 PREPARATION: 5 MINUTES PLUS
8 MINUTES COOKING TIME

 NUTRITION: GOOD SOURCE OF
VITAMIN C, FIBRE

Fruity Custard

••••••

1 pear, peeled, quartered and sliced
1 nectarine, peeled, stone removed and sliced
15ml (1 tbsp) orange juice
15ml (1 tbsp) water
15ml (1 tbsp) custard powder
10 ml (2tsp) sugar
150ml (¼ pint) full-fat milk

Place the fruit in a small saucepan with the orange juice and water.

Bring to the boil, reduce the heat, cover and simmer gently for 10 minutes or until the fruit is soft. Mash with a fork.

Meanwhile, blend the custard powder with the sugar and about two tablespoons of the milk. Mix in the remaining milk, transfer to a saucepan and heat, stirring continuously, until thickened and smooth.

Stir in the mashed fruit. Allow to cool before serving.

MAKES:
6 PORTIONS

STORAGE: 24 HOURS IN THE FRIDGE;
4 WEEKS IN THE FREEZER

PREPARATION: 10 MINUTES PLUS
10 MINUTES COOKING TIME

NUTRITION: GOOD SOURCE OF
VITAMIN C, PROTEIN, CALCIUM

Mango Fool

●●●●●●

½ ripe mango
30ml (2 tbsp) plain Greek yoghurt

Slice through the mango either side of the stone. Peel, then cut the flesh into cubes.

Mash or purée with a hand-held blender or in a food processor or blender until smooth.

Stir in the yoghurt.

 MAKES:
3 PORTIONS

 STORAGE: 24 HOURS IN THE FRIDGE;
4 WEEKS IN THE FREEZER

 PREPARATION:
10 MINUTES

 NUTRITION: GOOD SOURCE OF VITAMINS A
(BETA-CAROTENE) AND C, CALCIUM

Strawberry Yoghurt

●●●●●●

4–5 ripe strawberries
30ml (2 tbsp) plain whole milk or Greek yoghurt
5ml (1 tsp) orange juice

Wash the strawberries and pass through a sieve to remove the pips.

Combine with the yoghurt and orange juice.

MAKES:
1–2 PORTIONS

STORAGE: 24 HOURS IN THE FRIDGE;
4 WEEKS IN THE FREEZER

PREPARATION:
5 MINUTES

NUTRITION: GOOD SOURCE OF
VITAMIN C, CALCIUM

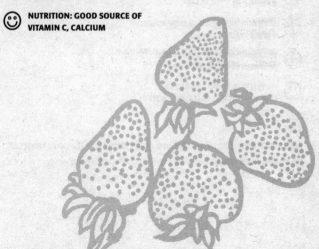

Banana Rice Pudding

●●●●●●

60g (2 oz) pudding (short grain) rice
600ml (1 pint) full-fat milk
15ml (1 tbsp) sugar (optional)
1 ripe banana

Put the rice, milk and sugar in a heavy-bottomed saucepan. Bring to the boil, reduce the heat and simmer for about 30 minutes, stirring occasionally.

Roughly mash the banana and combine with the rice pudding.

Serve lukewarm or cold.

MAKES:
6 PORTIONS

STORAGE: 24 HOURS IN THE FRIDGE;
4 WEEKS IN THE FREEZER

PREPARATION: 5 MINUTES PLUS
30 MINUTES COOKING TIME

NUTRITION: GOOD SOURCE OF
CARBOHYDRATE, CALCIUM, PROTEIN

TIP
Try using tinned apricots instead of the bananas. Choose apricots tinned in juice and mash the fruit roughly before serving.

Orchard Fruit Pudding

●●●●●●

1 eating apple, peeled, quartered and sliced
2 ripe plums, stoned and quartered
30ml (2 tbsp) water
60ml (4 tbsp) plain whole milk or Greek yoghurt

Put the apples and plums in a small saucepan with the water. Bring
to the boil, reduce the heat, cover and simmer for 5 minutes until
the fruit is soft.

Mash or purée the fruit. Combine with the yoghurt.

MAKES:
4 PORTIONS

STORAGE: 24 HOURS IN THE FRIDGE;
4 WEEKS IN THE FREEZER

PREPARATION:
10 MINUTES

NUTRITION: GOOD SOURCE OF
CALCIUM, POTASSIUM, VITAMIN C

Chapter 5
From Nine to Twelve Months

By now your baby will probably have a few teeth and be able to bite and chew. Solid food now becomes more important as a nutritional source. As your baby starts eating more food he or she will gradually take less milk at mealtimes and may drop some feeds altogether. Be guided by your baby's appetite.

CONTINUE TO INTRODUCE NEW FOODS

Your baby is ready for more intense flavours and different textures so it is important to offer as much variety as possible. Many experts believe that a unique window of opportunity exists around this time when your baby will readily accept new foods. If your baby's diet is fairly limited at this critical stage, it will be harder to encourage him or her to try new foods later on. So be warned!

Try sharper fruits, such as raspberries (sieved) or clementines, tomatoes, tuna and oily fish (check carefully for bones), mashed cooked beans (canned in water) and whole egg (cooked until white and yolk are firm). Most babies will enjoy garlic and herbs and mildly spiced food.

AIM FOR THREE MEALS A DAY

Your baby's meals can be fitted into the family routine, with
a couple of courses at each meal. Offer healthy snacks and drink
in between meals (see 'Snacks') plus milk at bedtime.

EAT AS A FAMILY

Your baby can now enjoy many of the same meals as the rest of the
family. At this stage baby foods don't need to be puréed. Simply
mash or chop your baby's portion but do not add salt. Avoid salty
ingredients such as stock cubes, ready-made sauces and soup
mixes. The social side of eating is an important part of your baby's
development so let him or her join in as much as possible.

ENCOURAGE SELF-FEEDING

Let your baby feed him or herself (be prepared for a mess!),
but don't offer help unless your baby seems frustrated.

GIVE LOTS OF WATER

The best drinks are cooled boiled water or well-diluted pure fruit
juice (one part juice to at least two or three parts of water). These
should not replace the usual milk feeds (see p 104). Offer drinks
in a cup or beaker.

Tip

Allow plenty of time for meals and don't expect your baby to eat properly when you are in a rush.

Make meals fun – serve in colourful bowls and plates, offer food with contrasting colours and shapes. It's amazing what babies will like. When Rosie was a baby she grabbed a piece of lemon from my glass of lemonade and started sucking it. Her wee face was all screwed up but the next time I had a slice of lemon in my drink she did it again, so she must have liked the sharp, sour taste!

HOW MUCH MILK?

Aim to give your baby around 500–600 ml of milk a day, either as a drink , as yoghurt, on cereals or in dishes. Give milk after a meal, say mid-morning or mid-afternoon, otherwise it may take the edge off your baby's appetite for food.

FUSSY EATING

Between nine and twelve months some babies start to exert their independence and refuse foods they previously liked. Try to be patient without showing concern – although that can often be hard when you have spent time making nutritious meals! The best thing to do is take the food away and try offering the same thing another day. You cannot force your baby to eat and persisting too much will only lead to confrontation and frustration. It may even put your baby off trying new foods again. Encouragement and gentle persuasion will help to avoid fussy eating (see 'Feeding Your Fussy Eater', page 154–157). Remember, though, that teething and your baby's overall well-being can also influence likes and dislikes from day to day.

Tip
Set a good example – eat together whenever you can and let your baby see you enjoying your food.

Tip
It is no longer necessary to sterilise every utensil your baby uses. You should, however, continue to sterilise bottles and teats as they are more difficult to clean thoroughly.

FINGER FOODS

From about nine months babies can use their thumb and forefinger to pick up foods. Offer your baby finger foods that are fun to eat. Make them into interesting shapes, perhaps with a dip (see recipes pages 113–116 and page 138). Hard finger foods also help ease sore gums when they are teething. Try the following:
• Baby tomatoes
• Carrot sticks
• Cooked broccoli or cauliflower florets
• Cooked baby corn
• Cooked mangetout
• Apple and pear slices
• Long slices of banana
• Cubes of cheese
• Soldiers of bread or toast
• Toasted triangles or strips of pitta bread or chapatti
• Rice cakes and crackers (unsalted)
• Raisins
• Cooked white, green and red pasta shapes

SNACKS

Once your baby is on the move, he or she will be burning more energy so will need frequent meals to satisfy his or her needs. Most babies can manage only small meals so you should offer two or three healthy snacks in between meals. Encourage your baby to snack on fruit and simple savouries rather than biscuits and sugar-laden snacks. These are safer for your baby's teeth and will also provide valuable nutrients. Here are some suggestions:

- Fresh fruit e.g. apple slices, orange segments, kiwi fruit
- Cubes of cheese
- Small pots or yoghurt or fromage frais
- Toast fingers with butter
- Carrots and cucumber sticks
- Unsalted crackers and rice cakes
- Breadsticks
- Mini sandwiches with savoury fillings

SUITABLE FOODS FROM NINE TO TWELVE MONTHS

Foods to include:	Foods to avoid:
• Cereals (including wheat), bread, pasta	• Added sugar as far as possible
• All fruit and vegetables	• Salt
• Lean meat, fish, poultry	• Processed (salty) meat products e.g. sausages, bacon, burgers, nuggets
• Beans, lentils and peas	• Crisps and salty snacks
• Milk and dairy products	• Sweets
• Whole eggs (cooked)	• Sugary foods and drinks e.g. biscuits, cakes, squash (occasional is fine)
	• Nuts
	• Mould-ripened soft cheese (e.g. Brie) and blue cheese
	• Honey
	• Uncooked eggs

WHAT YOUR BABY DOESN'T NEED

Salt
Don't add salt to your baby's food and avoid giving salty food for the first year. Babies' kidneys are immature and cannot cope with it. Salt can cause your baby to become dehydrated and lead to high blood pressure later in life. Avoid salty snacks (crisps, etc.), stock cubes, ready-made sauces and soups, ketchup, sauce mixes, ham, bacon, yeast extract and adult ready meals. Check the label for salt or sodium.

Sugar
Added sugar is unnecessary. It can cause diarrhoea in young babies and, in older babies and toddlers, is a major cause of tooth decay. Sugar and sugary foods provide empty calories – satisfying your baby's appetite but providing no other nutrients. They can also lead to a sweet tooth as your baby becomes accustomed to sweet-tasting foods. Encourage your baby to enjoy the natural sweetness in fresh fruit. Avoid products containing sugar, sucrose, glucose, glucose syrup, fructose, dextrose corn syrup, and invert sugar. Foods containing artificial sweeteners should not be given to children under three years old.

Honey
Honey is not recommended for babies under one year because it may contain botulism spores, which can cause food poisoning.

Wheat
Wheat, rye and oats contain gluten, a protein that can cause coeliac disease in a small number of babies if fed to them under the age of six months. Do not give your baby bread, pasta, breakfast cereals (except those for babies under six months), biscuits, breadsticks or any product containing these cereals.

Uncooked eggs
Uncooked eggs are not suitable for babies because of the small risk of salmonella infection. Egg yolk can be given after six months and whole eggs after nine months provided they are cooked until the yolk and white are solid.

Pâté, blue and soft ripened cheese
Pâté, blue cheese and soft ripened cheeses such as Brie and Camembert should not be given to babies under one year because of the risk of listeria.

VEGETARIAN BABIES

A vegetarian diet can be perfectly healthy for babies and toddlers. The early stages of weaning are just the same as for any other baby but after six months it is important to ensure your baby is getting all the nutrients that meat and fish would otherwise supply. The main nutrients to check are protein, iron and zinc.

Protein – Mixing pulses, such as lentils and beans, together with grains such as rice or pasta improves the protein value of the meal. Start with only small portions of pulses as they can be quite filling for small babies. Gradually increase the quantities as your baby gets older and develops a greater capacity for food. Dairy products and eggs also provide protein.

Iron – Pulses, eggs, green leafy vegetables, dried fruit and fortified baby cereals are good sources of iron. Including vitamin C-rich foods (such as fruit) at the same time increases iron absorption.

Zinc – Pulses, wholemeal bread and egg yolk supply zinc. For older babies over one year with no allergy history, ground nuts or nut butters are an important source of iron and zinc.

A vegan diet that also excludes dairy products and eggs may be too bulky for young babies. Contact your health visitor for advice and also the Vegan Society (address at end of book).

MEAL PLANNER –
FROM NINE TO TWELVE MONTHS

WEEK 1	DAY 1
Breakfast+	Instant porridge* with apple purée
Mid-morning	Breast or formula milk
Lunch	Vegetable and cheese pasta (p 118); Banana custard (p 142)
Mid-afternoon	Breast or formula milk
Tea+	Great dippers (p 113) with cheesy dip (p 116); Fruit
Bedtime	Breast or formula milk

WEEK 1	DAY 2
Breakfast+	Whole-wheat bisk** with mashed banana
Mid-morning	Breast or formula milk
Lunch	Mini meatballs in tomato sauce (p 124); Cauliflower; Fresh Fruit
Mid-afternoon	Breast or formula milk
Tea+	Mini pizza (p 120) with peas; Yoghurt
Bedtime	Breast or formula milk

WEEK 1	DAY 3
Breakfast+	Baby cereal with fresh fruit
Mid-morning	Breast or formula milk
Lunch	Mini fish cakes (p 122); Broccoli Fruit juice jelly
Mid-afternoon	Breast or formula milk
Tea+	Fun pasta (p 117); Fruit
Bedtime	Breast or formula milk

WEEK 1	DAY 4
Breakfast+	Instant porridge* with fresh fruit
Mid-morning	Breast or formula milk
Lunch	Lamb and vegetable casserole (p 126); Potato; Yoghurt
Mid-afternoon	Breast or formula milk
Tea+	Hummus (p 114) with great dippers (p 113) or toast fingers; Fruit dippers (p 138)
Bedtime	Breast or formula milk

WEEK 1	DAY 5
Breakfast+	Baby cereal with apricot purée
Mid-morning	Breast or formula milk
Lunch	Lentil and vegetable hotpot (p 136); Raspberry yoghurt (p 139)
Mid-afternoon	Breast or formula milk
Tea+	Mini sandwiches; Rice pudding with fruit (p 143)
Bedtime	Breast or formula milk

WEEK 1	DAY 6
Breakfast+	Well-cooked scrambled
Mid-morning	Breast or formula milk
Lunch	Creamy chicken and vegetables (p 130); Fruit dippers and yoghurt (p 138)
Mid-afternoon	Breast or formula milk
Tea+	Fish and broccoli supper (p 132); Fromage frais
Bedtime	Breast or formula milk

WEEK 1	DAY 7
Breakfast+	Toast fingers; fromage frais
Mid-morning	Breast or formula milk
Lunch	Baby's shepherd's pie (p 134); Fruit
Mid-afternoon	Breast or formula milk
Tea+	Pasta with creamy mushroom sauce (p 128); Bananas on toast (p 140)
Bedtime	Breast or formula milk

+ With a drink of cooled boiled water or well-diluted fruit juice
  (1 part juice with at least 2 parts water)

* Ready Brek or a similar oat cereal

** Weetabix or a similar wheat cereal with no added sugar

Your baby may not need a milk feed on waking but do listen to your baby's
individual needs

RECIPES
FOR BABIES
FROM NINE
MONTHS
●●●●●●●●●

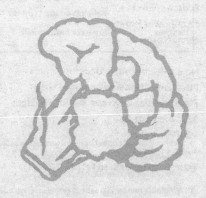

Great Dippers
●●●●●●●●●

Vegetable crudités dunked into a tasty dip are a great way of encouraging your baby's independence at mealtimes and improving hand-mouth co-ordination. It is also a fun way to eat vegetables!

Choose from the following:
Carrot sticks
Cucumber sticks
Cherry tomatoes
Red or yellow pepper strips
Courgette strips

The following may be lightly cooked to make them easier to eat:
French beans
Baby sweetcorn
Broccoli florets
Cauliflower florets
Mangetout

Here are some other ideas for dippers:
Pitta bread (toasted), cut into strips
Flour tortillas or wraps, cut into wedges
Mini breadsticks
Mini rice cakes
Toast soldiers
Thin slices of toasted French bread

Hummus

●●●●●●●●●

1 tin (400g) chickpeas (no added salt or sugar),
drained and rinsed
1 garlic clove
15ml (1 tbsp) olive oil
30ml (2 tbsp) tahini (sesame seed paste)
A little freshly squeezed lemon juice
15ml (1 tbsp) plain yoghurt

Place the drained chickpeas, garlic, tahini, lemon juice and yoghurt
in a blender. Blend to a smooth consistency.

Store covered in the fridge for up to 3 days and serve with crudités.

 MAKES:
8 PORTIONS

 **STORAGE: 3 DAYS
IN THE FRIDGE**

 PREPARATION:
5 MINUTES

 **NUTRITION: GOOD SOURCE OF
PROTEIN, FIBRE, IRON**

TIP

*It really is worth making your own hummus – ready-made versions
contain a lot of salt – and this recipe takes only minutes to prepare!*

Avocado Dip
●●●●●●●●●

1 ripe avocado
15ml (1 tbsp) lemon juice
1 small clove of garlic, crushed (optional)

Cut the avocado in half, remove the stone and scoop out the flesh. Mash the flesh with the lemon juice and garlic (if using).

Store covered in the fridge for up to 3 days and serve with crudités.

 MAKES:
4 PORTIONS

 STORAGE: 3 DAYS
IN THE FRIDGE

 PREPARATION:
5 MINUTES

☺ **NUTRITION: GOOD SOURCE OF**
VITAMIN E, MONOUNSATURATED FAT

TIP
The lemon juice stops the avocado discolouring.

Cheesy Dip

●●●●●●●●●

30g (1 oz) Edam or Cheddar cheese
15ml (1 tbsp) full-fat soft cheese or cream cheese
5ml (1 tsp) single cream or full-fat milk

Grate the cheddar cheese very finely. Add the full-fat soft cheese
and cream or milk and beat together until smooth.

 MAKES:
2–4 PORTIONS

 STORAGE: 3 DAYS
IN THE FRIDGE

 PREPARATION:
5 MINUTES

☺ **NUTRITION: GOOD SOURCE OF**
PROTEIN, CALCIUM

TIP
For older babies and children, make the dip more interesting by
adding some finely chopped chives, parsley or spring onions.

Fun Pasta

●●●●●●●●●

60g (2 oz) pasta shapes
Handful of cherry tomatoes, halved
30g (1 oz) mangetout
½ small red pepper, diced
30ml (2 tbsp) sweetcorn
15ml (1 tbsp) mayonnaise

Cook the pasta in plenty of boiling water according to the
directions on the packet. Add the mangetout and red pepper
during the last 2 minutes of cooking. Drain.

Place the pasta, red pepper and mangetout in a bowl. Add the
sweetcorn and mayonnaise and combine well.

Serve lukewarm or cold.

 MAKES:
2–3 PORTIONS

 STORAGE: 3 DAYS
IN THE FRIDGE

 PREPARATION: 10 MINUTES PLUS
10 MINUTES COOKING TIME

 NUTRITION: GOOD SOURCE OF VITAMIN C,
COMPLEX CARBOHYDRATES, FIBRE

TIP
*Your baby will enjoy picking up the different vegetables and pasta
shapes and feeding himself. Vary the ingredients according to your
baby's likes and dislikes – try peas, broccoli florets, chopped
cooked chicken or cubes of cheese.*

Vegetable and Cheese Pasta

•••••••••

1 carrot, peeled and sliced
3 spears broccoli
Handful of French beans, trimmed and
cut into 1–2-cm (½-inch) lengths
60g (2 oz) small pasta shapes
Cheese sauce:
22.5ml (1½ tbsp) butter or margarine
22.5ml (1½ tbsp) plain flour
175ml (6 fl oz) full fat milk
45ml (3 tbsp) Cheddar cheese, grated

Bring a little water to the boil in a small saucepan. Add the vegetables, reduce the heat and simmer for 10 minutes. Drain.

Meanwhile cook the pasta in plenty of boiling water according to the instructions on the packet. Drain.

Meanwhile, melt the butter or margarine in a small saucepan, stir in the flour and slowly add the milk, stirring continuously until the sauce thickens. Turn down the heat and simmer for a minute.

Remove the saucepan from the heat and stir in the grated cheese.

Add the cooked vegetables and pasta to the cheese sauce and stir well.

Mash or cut up small before serving lukewarm.

MAKES:
4–6 PORTIONS

STORAGE: 24 HOURS IN THE FRIDGE;
4 WEEKS IN THE FREEZER

PREPARATION: 10 MINUTES PLUS
10 MINUTES COOKING TIME

NUTRITION: GOOD SOURCE OF
VITAMINS A AND C, PROTEIN, CALCIUM

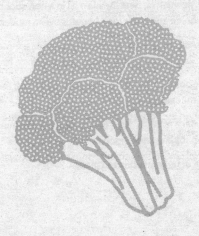

Mini Pizzas

● ● ● ● ● ● ● ● ● ●

1 English muffin, wholemeal or white
30 g (1 oz) Cheddar cheese, grated

Tomato sauce:
10ml (2 tsp) olive oil
1/2 onion, finely chopped
1/2 garlic clove, crushed
60ml (4 tbsp) passata (smooth sieved tomatoes)
or tinned chopped tomatoes
5ml (1 tsp) tomato purée
Pinch of dried basil

Split the muffin in half horizontally and toast the cut side under a hot grill.

Meanwhile, heat the olive oil in a non-stick pan and sauté the onion and garlic for 5 minutes over a moderate heat.

Add the passata or chopped tomatoes, tomato purée and basil. Simmer for 5–10 minutes until the sauce has thickened a little.

Spoon a little sauce over each muffin half then scatter the grated cheese over the top.

Bake at 200°C/400°F/Gas mark 6 for 10 minutes until the cheese is bubbling and golden brown.

Cut up into bite-sized pieces.

MAKES:
2 PORTIONS

STORAGE: 3 DAYS IN THE FRIDGE;
4 WEEKS IN THE FREEZER

PREPARATION: 10 MINUTES PLUS
20 MINUTES COOKING TIME

NUTRITION: GOOD SOURCE OF COMPLEX
CARBOHYDRATES, PROTEIN, CALCIUM

TIP
You could also use mini pitta breads, toasted halved baps or thick
slices of French bread for these simple pizzas. Add extra toppings
such as sliced tomatoes, strips of peppers, sweetcorn, peas or
flaked tuna.

Mini Fish Cakes

●●●●●●●●●

450g (1 lb) potatoes, peeled and chopped
225g (8 oz) salmon or cod fillet, skin removed (or 1 x 200g (7 oz)
tin salmon or tuna in oil or spring water)
Milk for poaching
30g (1 oz) butter
60ml (4 tbsp) milk
15ml (1 tbsp) fresh parsley, chopped

Place the potatoes in a saucepan of boiling water and cook for
12–15 minutes until soft. Drain.

Meanwhile, place the fish in a pan with enough milk to cover the
fish. Bring to the boil, reduce the heat and simmer for 5–10
minutes. Drain and flake the fish, carefully removing all the bones.

Mash the potatoes with the butter, milk and parsley. Mix in the
flaked fish. Shape into 8 small burgers or 'cakes'.

Heat a little olive oil in a frying pan and shallow fry the fish cakes for
a few minutes on each side until golden brown. You may need to
do this in 2 batches. Drain on kitchen paper.

MAKES:
8 PORTIONS

STORAGE: 3 DAYS IN THE FRIDGE;
4 WEEKS IN THE FREEZER

PREPARATION: 20 MINUTES PLUS
25 MINUTES COOKING TIME

NUTRITION: GOOD SOURCE OF PROTEIN, COMPLEX CARBOHYDRATES,
B VITAMINS, ESSENTIAL (OMEGA-3) FATS (SALMON)

TIP

These home-made fish cakes are far healthier than ready -made
versions, which can contain a lot of salt and flavour enhancers.
Make a larger quantity and freeze for quick meals at a later date.

Mini Meatballs in Tomato Sauce

●●●●●●●●●

Meatballs:
125g (4 oz) lean minced beef, pork or lamb
1/2 onion, finely chopped
30g (1 oz) mushrooms, finely chopped
15g (1/2 oz) fresh breadcrumbs
1 egg

Tomato sauce:
10ml (2 tbsp) olive oil
1/2 onion, finely chopped
1/2 garlic clove, crushed
60ml (4 tbsp) passata (smooth sieved tomatoes)
or tinned chopped tomatoes
5ml (1 tsp) tomato purée
2 1/2 ml (1/2 tsp) dried mixed herbs

To make the meatballs, combine all of the ingredients in a bowl or a blender until you have formed a smooth mixture. Divide and shape the mixture into small walnut-sized balls. Chill in the fridge while you make the sauce.

Heat the olive oil in a non-stick pan and sauté the onion and garlic for 5 minutes over a moderate heat.

Add the passata or chopped tomatoes, tomato purée and herbs. Simmer for 5–10 minutes until the sauce has thickened a little.

Heat a little oil in a frying pan over a moderate heat.

Fry the meatballs, turning frequently until they are lightly browned all over, about 5–10 minutes. Pour the sauce over the meatballs, part cover the pan and simmer for about 10 minutes.

MAKES: 10–12
BALLS OR 4 PORTIONS

STORAGE: 24 HOURS IN THE FRIDGE;
4 WEEKS IN THE FREEZER

PREPARATION: 20 MINUTES PLUS
30 MINUTES COOKING TIME

NUTRITION: GOOD SOURCE OF PROTEIN,
IRON, BETA-CAROTENE (VITAMIN A)

TIP
Meatballs are a classic children's favourite. You can serve this healthy version with a ready-made tomato (pasta) sauce to save time or mix with cheese sauce or a vegetable sauce for a change.

Lamb and Vegetable Casserole

●●●●●●●●●●

15ml (1 tbsp) sunflower oil
1 small onion, chopped
2 small lamb cutlets
30ml (2 tbsp) of flour
1 x 400g (13 oz) tin chopped tomatoes
2 potatoes, peeled and diced
2 carrots, peeled and sliced
125g (4 oz) peas
150ml (¼ pint) vegetable stock (see page 21) or water

This can be cooked in a pan on the top of the stove or in the oven.

Heat the oil in a large pan. Add the onions and cook for about 5 minutes.

Cut the meat into small pieces then toss in the flour. Add to the pan, stir for a few minutes until the meat browns.

Add the tomatoes, potatoes, carrots, peas and stock or water and bring to the boil. Reduce the heat, cover and simmer for about one hour either in the pan or in a casserole dish in the oven (180°C/350°F/Gas mark 4).

Serve lukewarm, chopped small for younger babies.

MAKES:
4 PORTIONS

 STORAGE: 24 HOURS IN THE FRIDGE;
4 WEEKS IN THE FREEZER

 PREPARATION: 15 MINUTES PLUS
1 HOUR COOKING TIME

 NUTRITION: GOOD SOURCE OF PROTEIN,
IRON, BETA-CAROTENE (VITAMIN A)

TIP

You can use beef or pork instead of the lamb and other vegetables
that your baby likes. Try sliced peppers, swede or sweet potatoes.

Pasta with Creamy Mushroom Sauce

•••••••••

60g (2 oz) pasta shapes
15ml (1 tbsp) olive oil
1 small onion, chopped
60g (2 oz) button mushrooms, chopped
1 garlic clove, crushed
10ml (2 tsp) cornflour
125ml (4 fl oz) full-fat milk
Fresh parsley, chopped

Cook the pasta in plenty of boiling water according to the directions on the packet. Drain.

Meanwhile, heat the olive oil in a non-stick pan over a moderate heat. Add the onions, mushrooms and garlic and cook for about 5 minutes or until soft.

Mix the cornflour with a little of the milk in a small jug. Add the remaining milk to the jug, stirring well. Slowly add to the mushroom mixture, stirring continuously until the sauce has thickened.

Combine the sauce with the cooked pasta. Roughly mash to a lumpy consistency with a fork. Serve this dish lukewarm with broccoli or carrots to balance the meal.

MAKES:
2–3 PORTIONS

 STORAGE: 24 HOURS IN THE FRIDGE;
4 WEEKS IN THE FREEZER

 PREPARATION: 10 MINUTES PLUS
10 MINUTES COOKING TIME

 NUTRITION: GOOD SOURCE OF
COMPLEX CARBOHYDRATES, CALCIUM

TIP

Mushrooms mixed with a creamy sauce are a good way of
introducing this vegetable to your baby.

Creamy Chicken and Vegetables

●●●●●●●●●●

1 carrot, peeled and sliced
2 spears of broccoli
2 florets cauliflower
15g ($^1/_2$ oz) butter or margarine
15ml (1 tbsp) plain flour
125 ml (4 fl oz) full-fat milk
30g (1 oz) Cheddar cheese, grated
60g (2 oz) cooked chicken, cut into small pieces

Bring a little water to the boil in a small saucepan and add the vegetables. Reduce the heat, cover and simmer for 10 minutes or until tender.

Meanwhile, melt the butter or margarine in a small saucepan, stir in the flour and slowly add the milk, stirring continuously until the sauce thickens. Turn down the heat and simmer for a minute.

Remove the saucepan from the heat and stir in the grated cheese.

Mix the vegetables and chicken in to the cheese sauce. Roughly mash or cut up small and serve lukewarm.

MAKES:
4 PORTIONS

 STORAGE: 24 HOURS IN THE FRIDGE;
4 WEEKS IN THE FREEZER

 PREPARATION: 15 MINUTES PLUS
10 MINUTES COOKING TIME

 NUTRITION: GOOD SOURCE OF PROTEIN,
VITAMIN C, CALCIUM

TIP

Combining vegetables with a cheese sauce makes them more appealing to babies. You can use other varieties of vegetables, such as courgettes or cabbage, or substitute flaked cooked fish for the chicken.

Fish and Broccoli Supper

●●●●●●●●●

125–175g (4–6 oz) **white fish fillet**
(e.g. cod, plaice, coley)
45–60ml (3–4 tbsp) **full-fat milk**
3 spears **broccoli**
15g (¹/₂ oz) **butter or margarine**
15ml (1 tbsp) **plain flour**
125ml (4 fl oz) **full-fat milk**
45g (1¹/₂ oz) **Cheddar cheese, grated**

Place the fish in a small saucepan and pour over the milk. Bring to
the boil, reduce the heat, part cover the pan and simmer for about
10 minutes until the fish is cooked.

Remove the fish from the milk using a slotted spoon, flake and
roughly mash with a fork, carefully removing any bones.

Meanwhile, cook the broccoli in a little water for 5–7 minutes
until just tender.

To make the sauce, melt the butter or margarine in a small
saucepan, stir in the flour and slowly add the milk, stirring
continuously until the sauce thickens. Turn down the heat and
simmer for a minute.

Remove the saucepan from the heat and stir in the grated cheese,
broccoli and fish.

Mash roughly with a fork and serve lukewarm.

MAKES:
4 PORTIONS

STORAGE: 24 HOURS IN THE FRIDGE;
4 WEEKS IN THE FREEZER

PREPARATION: 10 MINUTES PLUS
10 MINUTES COOKING TIME

NUTRITION: GOOD SOURCE OF
PROTEIN, CALCIUM, VITAMIN C

TIP

Broccoli is a rich source of vitamin C, folic acid and iron.

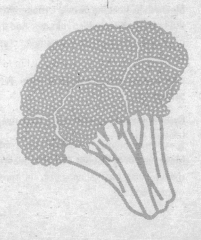

Baby's Shepherd's Pie

●●●●●●●●●

400g (1 lb) potatoes, peeled and chopped
125g (4 oz) parsnip or swede,
peeled and chopped (optional)
15ml (1 tbsp) olive oil
1 small onion, finely chopped
1 carrot, peeled and grated
125g (4 oz) lean minced beef or lamb
30ml (2 tbsp) chopped tinned tomatoes
125ml (4 fl oz) chicken stock (unsalted) or water
45ml (3 tbsp) full-fat milk

Bring a little water to the boil in a saucepan. Add the potatoes and parsnip or swede (if using), reduce the heat, cover and simmer for about 10–15 minutes until tender.

Meanwhile, heat the oil over a moderate heat in a frying pan, add the onion and sauté for 5 minutes. Add the carrots and minced meat and continue cooking, stirring occasionally, until the meat is browned.

Add the tomatoes and stock or water and simmer for about 20 minutes.

Drain then mash the potatoes and parsnip or swede with the milk.

For younger babies, mix the meat and potato mixture together and mash until fairly smooth. For older babies and children, spoon the meat mixture into a serving dish and spread the mashed potato mixture on top.

MAKES:
4–6 PORTIONS

STORAGE: 24 HOURS IN THE FRIDGE;
4 WEEKS IN THE FREEZER

PREPARATION: 10 MINUTES PLUS
30 MINUTES COOKING TIME

NUTRITION: GOOD SOURCE OF
PROTEIN, IRON, FIBRE

Lentil and Vegetable Hotpot

••••••••••

10ml (2 tsp) olive oil
1 small onion, chopped
1 garlic clove, crushed
1 carrot, peeled and sliced
1 potato, peeled and chopped
1/2 red pepper, peeled and chopped
45ml (3 tbsp) red lentils
300ml (1/2 pint) water
60g (2 oz) Cheddar cheese, grated

Heat the olive oil in a heavy-based saucepan. Add the onion, garlic, carrot, potato and pepper and sauté for about 5 minutes.

Add the lentils and water. Bring to the boil, cover and simmer for about 30 minutes or until the lentils are quite mushy. Top up with a little more water during cooking, if necessary.

Scatter over the grated cheese, mash roughly and serve lukewarm.

 MAKES:
4 PORTIONS

 STORAGE: 24 HOURS IN THE FRIDGE;
4 WEEKS IN THE FREEZER

 PREPARATION: 10 MINUTES PLUS
30 MINUTES COOKING TIME

 NUTRITION: GOOD SOURCE OF
PROTEIN, FIBRE, IRON, B VITAMINS

Baby Baked Potatoes

●●●●●●●●●

New potatoes
A little olive oil
Dried mixed herbs (optional)

Scrub and dry the new potatoes. Prick the skins and place them in a baking tin. Drizzle over a little olive oil, sprinkle over the herbs and roll the potatoes in the oil until they are well coated.

Bake in the oven (200°C/400°F/Gas mark 6) for 25–30 minutes or until they are tender.

Split the potatoes and fill with one of the following toppings:
Grated cheese
Cottage cheese
Tuna mixed with mayonnaise
Vegetables in a cheese sauce
Hummus (see page 114)
Creamy Mushroom Sauce
(see 'Pasta with Creamy Mushroom Sauce, page 128)
Creamy Chicken and Vegetables (see page 130)
Cheesy Lentil Savoury (see page 84)

 MAKES:
1 OR MORE PORTIONS

 STORAGE:
UNSUITABLE

 PREPARATION: 5 MINUTES PLUS
30 MINUTES COOKING TIME

 NUTRITION (NEW POTATOES): GOOD SOURCE OF
COMPLEX CARBOHYDRATES, VITAMIN C, FIBRE

Fruit Dippers and Yoghurt

●●●●●●●●●

Babies love dipping easy-to-hold pieces of fruit into creamy yoghurt. It is also a great way to encourage babies to feed themselves.

Choose seasonal fresh fruit, such as:

Apples, peeled and cut into thin slices
Nectarine, peeled and thinly sliced
Banana, peeled and cut into chunks
Kiwi fruit, peeled and cut into slices
Pineapple rings
Mango, peeled and sliced
Strawberries, halved
Raspberries
Apricots, thinly sliced

Whole milk yoghurt or a 'baby' yoghurt (made without additives) or home-made raspberry yoghurt (see below).

Arrange the fruit attractively on a plate with a small bowl or pot of yoghurt.

TIP
This is a fun way to introduce your baby to new types of fruit.

Raspberry Yoghurt

●●●●●●●●●

125g (4 oz) raspberries
60ml (4 tbsp) plain whole milk or Greek yoghurt
10ml (2 tsp) orange juice

Press the raspberries through a sieve to remove the pips.

Combine the purée with the yoghurt and orange juice.

MAKES:
2 PORTIONS

STORAGE: 24 HOURS IN THE FRIDGE;
4 WEEKS IN THE FREEZER

PREPARATION:
5 MINUTES

NUTRITION: GOOD SOURCE OF
VITAMIN C, PROTEIN, CALCIUM

Bananas on Toast

●●●●●●●●●

5ml (1 tsp) butter
1 ripe banana, peeled and thickly sliced
Pinch of cinnamon
1 fruit bun (wholemeal or white)

Melt the butter in a small heavy-bottomed pan. Add the banana slices and cook for 1 minute, turning gently.

Add the honey and cinnamon and continue cooking for 2 minutes until softened.

Split the fruit bun and toast under a hot grill. Spoon over the banana mixture.

Cut into bite-sized pieces to serve.

 MAKES:
2 PORTIONS

 STORAGE:
UNSUITABLE

 PREPARATION: 5 MINUTES PLUS
3 MINUTES COOKING TIME

 NUTRITION: GOOD SOURCE OF
CARBOHYDRATE, FIBRE, VITAMIN B6

TIP
Instead of the fruit bun, you can use slices of toasted raisin bread, wholemeal or white bread or English muffins.

Fruit Juice Jelly

●●●●●●●●●

300ml (½ pint) fruit juice, e.g. orange, apple
10ml (2 tsp) powdered gelatine

Place 60ml (4 tbsp) of the fruit juice in a small bowl. Sprinkle the gelatine over the juice and leave to soak for 5 minutes. Place over a pan of boiling water and stir the mixture until the gelatine has dissolved.

Remove from the heat and stir into the rest of the juice.

Divide into 2 or 3 individual dishes and place in the fridge for a few hours (or overnight) until the gelatine has set.

 MAKES:
2–3 PORTIONS

 STORAGE: 2 DAYS
IN THE FRIDGE

 PREPARATION:
10 MINUTES

 NUTRITION: GOOD SOURCE OF
VITAMIN C, POTASSIUM

Banana Custard

●●●●●●●●●●

15ml (1 tbsp) custard powder
10ml (2 tsp) sugar
150ml (¹/₄ pint) full-fat milk
1 ripe banana

Blend the custard powder with the sugar and about 30ml (2 tbsp) of the milk. Mix in the remaining milk, transfer to a saucepan and heat, stirring continuously, until thickened and smooth.

Slice the banana and stir into the custard. Allow to cool before serving.

 MAKES:
2–3 PORTIONS

 STORAGE: 24 HOURS
IN THE FRIDGE

 PREPARATION:
5 MINUTES

 NUTRITION: GOOD SOURCE OF
CALCIUM, PROTEIN, FIBRE

TIP
Try making this with other varieties of stewed fresh or tinned fruit – tinned apricots or pineapple, stewed apples, rhubarb or pears.

Rice Pudding with Fruit

●●●●●●●●●●

Rice pudding:
60g (2 oz) pudding (short grain) rice
600ml (1 pint) full-fat milk
15ml (1 tbsp) sugar (optional)
5ml (1 tsp) vanilla extract

Choose from the following fruit:
Stewed apples or pears
Stewed plums
Raspberries, blackberries or blueberries
Mango slices
Tinned apricots or peaches

Put the rice, milk and sugar in a heavy-bottomed saucepan. Bring to the boil, reduce the heat and simmer for about 30 minutes, stirring occasionally.

Serve lukewarm or cold topped with the fruit.

 MAKES:
6 PORTIONS

 STORAGE: 24 HOURS IN THE FRIDGE;
4 WEEKS IN THE FREEZER

 PREPARATION: 5 MINUTES PLUS
30 MINUTES COOKING TIME

 NUTRITION: GOOD SOURCE OF PROTEIN,
CALCIUM, VITAMIN C AND FIBRE (FRUIT)

TIP
Instead of the fruit, you can serve the rice pudding with a spoonful of red fruit jam (ideally a low sugar jam), fruit spread or ready-made fruit compote.

Baby Food Guide – Summary

4 Months	
Number of meals per day	1, moving on to 2 mini-meals after 2 weeks
How much	1–6 teaspoons
Texture	Ultra smooth; fairly runny purées
Vegetables	Cooked potato, sweet potato, butternut squash, swede, parsnip, carrot, pumpkin
Fruit	Cooked apple and pear; well-mashed banana, papaya and avocado
Cereals	Baby rice, white rice, millet, polenta
Pulses	No
Dairy foods	No
Meat	No
Fish	No
Nuts & Seeds	No
Milk	Breast milk or 600ml (1 pint) infant formula milk

5–6 Months

Number of meals per day	2 moving on to 3
How much	6–12 teaspoons
Texture	Smooth; slightly thicker purées
Vegetables	Stronger flavoured vegetables: cooked spinach, broccoli, courgette, cauliflower and peas
Fruit	Raw melon, mango, papaya, peaches, nectarines, blueberries; apricots and plums (cooked); dried apricots and peaches (cooked)
Cereals	As 4 months
Pulses	Small portions of cooked puréed red lentils mixed with vegetables
Dairy foods	Small portions of yoghurt and fromage frais
Meat	Tiny portions of puréed well-cooked chicken, turkey mixed with vegetables
Fish	No
Nuts & Seeds	No
Milk	Breast milk or 600ml (1 pint) infant formula milk

6–9 Months

Number of meals per day	3
How much	1–4 tablespoons
Texture	Thicker, lumpier purées or mashed food. Finger foods can be introduced
Vegetables	As 5 months plus sweetcorn, peppers, celery, cabbage, onion, leek, tomato
Fruit	Kiwi fruit, stoned cherries, strawberries, raspberries, blackberries, small amounts of cooked, puréed dried fruit (e.g. apricots, prunes, peaches)
Cereals	Wheat, pasta, bread, breakfast cereals (no added sugar), porridge, oats, barley
Pulses	Small portions of cooked, mashed beans and lentils
Dairy foods	Full-fat cow's milk on cereals or as part of a dish (but not as the main drink), mild hard cheese (e.g. Cheddar, Edam), hard-boiled egg yolk
Meat	As 5 months plus cooked, minced, lean meat
Fish	Cooked, flaked white fish (e.g. cod, plaice) and mild-tasting fish (e.g. salmon)
Nuts & Seeds	No
Milk	Breast milk or 600ml (1 pint) infant formula or follow-on milk

9–12 Months

Number of meals per day	3 plus 2 snacks
Texture	Mashed or finely chopped food Finger foods
Vegetables	Wide range of vegetables
Fruit	Wide range of fruit, diluted fruit juice (1 part juice: 2 or 3 parts water) as a drink
Cereals	Wide range of cereals but limit foods made with refined flour (biscuits, cakes)
Pulses	All types
Dairy foods	Increase variety but avoid blue or mould-ripened soft cheese, hard-boiled egg
Meat	Increase variety. Small portions of oily fish and stronger tasting fish (e.g. tuna, mackerel)
Nuts & Seeds	No
Milk	Breast milk or 600ml (1 pint) infant formula or follow-on milk

PART TWO
FEEDING YOUR TODDLER

Chapter 6
From Twelve Months

As babies grow into toddlers, their awareness of the world around them increases and they begin to exercise their independence. They also realise that they have more control over their surroundings and mealtimes are the perfect opportunity to test the boundaries. Some toddlers will eat virtually anything you give them but most go through phases of fussy eating, which can be very frustrating to say the least. Toddlers start to get clear opinions about what they will and won't eat, loving a certain food one day and disliking it the next. Their appetite can be equally unpredictable. You may well find that your previously good eater now picks at his or her food, refuses to eat or continually attempts to leave the table. Feeding a toddler often proves much more difficult than feeding a baby!

Here are some practical ways you can help your toddler to develop good eating habits and prevent mealtimes becoming a battleground.

BE A GOOD ROLE MODEL

Children learn by example so try to be a good role model by eating healthily yourself and eating together whenever possible. Let your toddler see you enjoying your food and he or she will soon develop good habits themselves. If children see you eating junk food or seldom sitting down at the table to eat, they are likely to do the same.

FAMILY MEALS

Try to eat together as a family whenever possible, even if you can only manage to do so at weekends. Children benefit from eating with other people and it helps them to develop their social skills. Your toddler can eat virtually all the same foods as the rest of the family – just make sure that they don't contain high amounts of sugar, salt or additives.

VARIED TASTES

Good eating habits are formed early so try to get your toddler used to trying new foods.

You can offer spicier food now, if you wish, and introduce nuts and seeds (ground or finely chopped) if there is no history of allergy in the family. Honey is also fine now but you should continue to avoid uncooked eggs and soft mould-ripened and blue cheeses.

Tip
Don't worry if your child doesn't finish the plate – it's more important that he or she eats a little of everything rather than nothing.

NO MORE MUSHY FOOD

You won't need to use the food processor any more, just cut the food into bite-sized pieces. It is a mistake to think that toddlers prefer bland mushy foods, now is the time to get them to appreciate the flavours and textures of real nutritious food.

AVOID 'CHILDREN'S' FOODS

Don't fall into the trap of giving your toddler 'children's' food –
burgers, nuggets, sausages, crisps, and puddings – every mealtime.
These foods are fine once in while but are, in fact, poor nutritional
value for money. Most are lacking in vitamins, minerals and fibre,
or contain high levels of sugar, salt, fat and artificial additives. What's
more, children quickly get used to the taste of processed food and
forget what real food should taste like! So when you present them with
fresh vegetables, for example, they are even less likely to eat them.

The recipe section gives you plenty of ideas for quick meals
that are made from healthy ingredients (see pages 166–253).

MAKE FOOD FUN

You can encourage your toddler to eat good food by presenting
the food imaginatively. You don't have to spend hours arranging
food in complicated shapes – just a simple pattern (such as a circle
or star) or an assortment of colours can make a big difference. Try
to choose different coloured and textured foods and arrange them
attractively on the plate. You can also make eating more fun with
bright coloured plates, cutlery and cups.

Tip
*Always get your toddler to sit down at the table to eat. Make
mealtimes important yet relaxed occasions – turn off the television
as this detracts from eating.*

EASY MEALS

Don't think that you always have to prepare traditional meals of meat and two veg. Many toddlers are happier with simple food that is easy and fun to eat – wholemeal toast soldiers, vegetable and fruit 'dippers' to dunk into interesting dips, cubes of cheese and small pots of yoghurt. As long as you provide a good balance of nutritious foods – fruit and vegetables, full-fat dairy products, protein foods and carbohydrate in the form of cereals or potatoes – they will get all the nutrients they need.

Tip
Ulrika Jonnson: I always took a banana in my bag when out and about in case Cameron and Bo got hungry.

SNACKING

Now they are on the move, toddlers burn more energy so their calorie and nutritional needs increase. Snacking is a good way to make sure they get enough of the right food. In addition to three meals a day, offer your toddler two or three nutritious snacks – slices of fresh fruit, mini sandwiches, raisins, yoghurt and cubes of cheese (see box on page 155).

But don't give in to demands for biscuits and crisps in the belief that 'it's better that they eat something rather than nothing'. Eating 'empty calories' between meals will simply take away your toddler's appetite for more nutritious foods at mealtimes and perpetuate a preference for salty and sugary processed foods. And there will be even less chance of your toddler getting the vitamins, minerals and other nutrients that they need.

Tip

For quite a long time I got away with giving Rosie those little boxes of raisins as a substitute for sweets. It doesn't really work once they go to school – and it is worth remembering that even raisins contain enough sugar to damage little teeth – but it's better than giving them a bar of chocolate.

MILK

Now that your toddler is eating a wider range of foods, milk becomes less important as a nutritional source. During the second year it is not necessary to use formula milk any more – full-fat cow's milk is fine. Make sure that your toddler gets about 350ml per day (or the equivalent in other dairy products). Skimmed milk is not recommended for under-fives because of its low calorie content but semi-skimmed milk can be given to toddlers over two provided they are getting enough calories from other foods.

FEEDING YOUR FUSSY EATER

Toddlers are entitled to dislike certain foods but some take this to extremes and are frustratingly fussy. When you have spent time and effort preparing food that your toddler refuses to eat, you will feel annoyed and resentful, but try not to make a big issue of this.

Toddlers are very good at using food to assert their independence and gain attention. The more firmly they refuse to eat a particular food, the more attention they get and a vicious circle's quickly set up.

Don't expect your toddler to 'grow out' of fussy eating – they won't! Most toddlers need to be trained to eat proper meals and nutritious food. It's not necessary to insist that they clear their plate

HEALTHY SNACKS

Fruit Snacks

Slices of apple or pear

Segments of satsumas or clementines

Red or white seedless grapes

Strawberries

Slices of nectarine

Chunks of banana

Small tins of fruit or fruit in jelly

Small boxes of raisins

Mini packets of dried apricots, mango, and tropical fruit mix

Bread/Cereal Snacks

(encourage wholemeal varieties if possible as they provide more B vitamins, iron and fibre than white)

Mini sandwiches

Toast fingers with butter/ Marmite/ honey/ jam

Breadsticks

Rice cakes

Crackers with cheese

Plain popcorn

Half a fruit bun/ hot cross bun/ muffin

Cereal or breakfast bar

Home-made cakes/ muffins

Dairy snacks

Pot of yoghurt or fromage frais

Yoghurt/ fromage frais pouches/ tubes

Individually wrapped mini cheeses

Cheese slices

Cheese snacks (e.g. Strip cheese, cheese strings)

Yoghurt drink

Foods to Avoid

Excessive sugar – occasional biscuits and cakes are fine but avoid giving sugary foods more than once daily

Added salt – limit salty foods such as crisps, salty snacks and ready-made sauces to twice weekly

Coffee and tea

Peanuts (only if there is a history of allergy in your family)

but you need to set your own boundaries at mealtimes. A clear strategy will help to persuade your toddler that food is enjoyable and fun. Ultimately, it will help your toddler to develop greater confidence around food. Here are some tips to help you cope with fussy eaters:

- Make sure your toddler is hungry before mealtimes – plenty of fresh air and exercise does wonders for the appetite.
- Avoid giving snacks too close to mealtimes.
- Allow your toddler to help with the shopping and the meal preparation. This will increase their interest in the food, and they will be more likely to eat the meal if they have been involved in making it.
- Try to eat together as a family whenever possible.
- Give your toddler the same food as everyone else.
- Serve small portions even if they seem ridiculously tiny to you – a big pile of food on the plate can be off-putting for toddlers. It's better that they eat a little than nothing at all.
- If your toddler refuses a meal, do not get cross but do not offer an alternative. Wait until the next scheduled snack or mealtime before offering food again.
- If you are introducing a new food make sure your toddler is hungry – that way, he or she is more likely to eat it.
- Don't force-feed your toddler – he or she will react to your concern by eating even less and even more slowly.
- Unpopular vegetables can sometimes be disguised – in soup, curries, or pasta sauce – but don't try and hide them under other foods otherwise you risk the whole meal being rejected.
- If your toddler rejects a food, it doesn't mean they will never eat it. Keep re-introducing those foods they reject, say once a week, and don't give up after two or three tries. It can take up to eight or ten attempts to get a child to eat a new food.
- Don't bargain with food, promising a favourite food or dessert only if he or she eats the refused one ('you can have your ice cream when you have eaten your vegetables') – this will only

reinforce the dislike of the refused food and make the other food seem more 'special'.

- Allow them to select their own food but from within a limited choice, e.g. 'would you like strawberry or apricot yoghurt?'
- If they refuse to eat their meal after the allocated time (say, 30 minutes), remove it without fuss and do not offer any other food until the next mealtime. Be consistent and rest assured that they won't become malnourished straight away. This won't be easy but they will soon realise that they only get food at mealtimes.

Tip

Don't get into the habit of feeding your toddler on the go (e.g. in the buggy or car) or in front of the TV. It will be harder to break later on.

WHEN YOUR TODDLER REFUSES TO EAT

Most toddlers go through a phase of refusing meals. Some can go for days or even weeks eating seemingly very little. The important thing to remember is that children will never starve themselves – when they are hungry enough they will eat.

There are a number of explanations:

- Your toddler may be teething – painful gums are enough to diminish the heartiest appetite.
- Your toddler may be coming down with a cold – a small appetite often accompanies minor infections.
- Your toddler may simply be too tired to eat.
- Your toddler is working out that saying no to food provokes a reaction.
- Your toddler may not be starving and could well be getting more than you realise. How much is your toddler drinking? Does your toddler have many snacks between meals? Drinks such as milk or

juice and snacks such as crisps and chocolate provide quite a lot of calories and may be taking the edge off your toddler's appetite for proper food. The solution is not to allow your toddler to fill up on too many drinks or give into your toddler's demands for snacks. Sooner or later your toddler will get the message that he or she has to eat at mealtimes.

If none the above reasons explain your toddler's eating behaviour and your toddler continues to refuse food that he or she has previously liked, have a chat with your health visitor or doctor in case there is a medical explanation.

Tip
Don't get cross with your toddler when he or she refuses to eat – that will make him even less likely to eat.

MY CHILD ONLY EATS MARMITE SANDWICHES!

Lots of toddlers go through a phase of eating only a very limited range of foods. Go along with it – it will eventually pass. In the meantime, if you are worried about your toddler's nutrition, give children's vitamin drops (see 'Vitamin Drops' page 74).

HELPING IN THE KITCHEN

Involving your toddler in food preparation can make mealtimes an opportunity for learning as well. Many children seem to enjoy helping in the kitchen and are more willing to eat foods that they have helped to prepare. Be patient, though, and be prepared for tasks to take longer than usual. Here are some suggestions:

2-year-olds can
Wipe table tops
Wash vegetables and fruit
Tear salad leaves
Bring ingredients from one place to another
Play with (non-breakable!) bowls, containers, spoons
Stir ingredients under supervision

3-year-olds can also:
Pour liquids
Spoon ingredients into a bowl
Mix ingredients
Wrap potatoes in foil
Roll pastry or biscuit dough
Cut out shapes with pastry/ biscuit cutters
Spread soft spreads
Assemble simple sandwiches

Tip
*Expect a bit of mess or a few accidents but at least you are
teaching your child valuable skills about food preparation.*

THE GOOD DRINK GUIDE

Toddlers need to drink enough fluids to prevent dehydration and
keep their bodies working properly. Even a small deficit can make
young children feel
• Lethargic
• Less able to play physically
• Less able to concentrate
• Generally unwell

Don't wait until your child complains of being thirsty. By this stage, he or she could already be slightly dehydrated. Try and make sure your toddler gets 6–8 (small) cups of drink a day, and more in hot weather.

Which drinks are best?

Encourage your toddler to drink water or milk as these drinks are the least harmful to young teeth. Discourage sugary drinks, such as squash and ready-made fruit drinks, because they can decay young teeth very easily. Diluted fruit juice (1 part juice to at least 2 parts water) is a better option.

It's worth knowing that all types of juices and soft drinks (including 'sugar-free' or 'low-sugar' drinks) can dissolve the soft enamel of children's teeth. They contain natural fruit acids, so are best confined to mealtimes. Cut the risk by encouraging your children to drink with a straw – this reduces the contact of the drink with the teeth.

Healthiest alternatives to water and milk include:

- Fruit juice diluted with water (1 part juice to at least 2 parts water)
- Organic squash or pure fruit cordial (well diluted) made without artificial additives
- Yoghurt drinks
- Milkshakes (see pages 238–244)

Tip

Don't use food as a bribe or a reward

VEGETARIAN TODDLERS

A vegetarian diet – one that excludes meat, poultry and fish – can definitely provide all the nutrients toddlers need to grow properly and keep perfectly healthy. Meat can easily be replaced with other sources of the nutrients that meat contains. The main ones to check are:

Protein – To get enough protein from a vegetarian diet, children need to eat a wide variety of plant proteins, for example pulses (such as beans, lentils and peas), soya products (such as tofu, soya burgers, soya milk), quorn products (such as quorn burgers and sausages), nuts, seeds and whole grain cereals (such as bread, pasta, rice). Dairy foods (milk, cheese, yoghurt, fromage frais) supply high-quality protein but you need to combine two or more plant foods to get the right balance of protein. Examples include: beans on toast, peanut butter sandwich, hummus with pitta fingers.

Iron – obtain from wholegrain bread and cereal foods, green leafy vegetables (broccoli, spinach), beans, lentils, nuts, seeds, and iron-fortified breakfast cereals. Offer a vitamin-C rich food or drink (e.g. fruit or fruit juice) at mealtimes to increase iron absorption.

Vitamin B12 – obtain from dairy foods or eggs or B12-fortified breakfast cereals and soya products.

Calcium – obtain from dairy foods, seeds, calcium-fortified soya products, almonds and oranges.

The recipe section (pages 166–253) includes many recipes suitable for vegetarian children.

Tip
Do not 'top them up' with biscuits or sweets after mealtimes. If they are still hungry, offer only nutritious foods, such as fruit, cheese or yoghurt.

TODDLER MEAL PLANNER

DAY 1

Breakfast+	Porridge* with banana
Lunch	Golden chicken fingers (p 174); Homemade chips (p 204), Broccoli; Fresh fruit slices
Tea+	Vegetable soup (p 192); Bread; Fromage frais

DAY 2

Breakfast+	Wholewheat bisk** with chopped fruit
Lunch	Speedy fish risotto (p 188); Summer fruit fool
Tea+	Mini sandwiches; Cucumber; Tomatoes Yoghurt

DAY 3

Breakfast+	Toast with honey Yoghurt
Lunch	Pasta bolognese (p 170); Fruit slices
Tea+	Baked beans on toast; Grated cheese; Fruit juice jelly (p 141)

DAY 4

Breakfast+	Shreddies/mini shredded wheats with fresh fruit
Lunch	Perfect baked potatoes (p 200); peas; Yoghurt
Tea+	Quick tomato pasta (p 208); Carrots; Fruit dippers (p 138)

DAY 5

Breakfast+	Toast fingers with Marmite; Cup of milk
Lunch	One-pot chicken casserole (p 172); Yoghurt
Tea+	Great dippers (p 113) with avocado dip (p 114) or mayonnaise; Rice pudding with fruit

DAY 6

Breakfast+	Banana shake (p 238)
Lunch	Easy fish cakes (p 190); Broccoli; Sweetcorn; Summer fruit fool (p 230)
Tea+	Boiled egg with toast fingers; Carrot batons; Fromage frais

DAY 7	
Breakfast+	Toasted muffin with well-cooked poached egg
Lunch	Toad 'n' Veg in the hole (p 166); Best apple crumble (p 234)
Tea+	Tuna wrap (p 203); Crudités; Fresh fruit slices

Plus:

2 snacks a day – see above (page 153)

6–8 cups of drink – see above (page 159–60)

+ With a drink of cooled boiled water or well-diluted fruit juice (1 part juice with at least 2 parts water)

* Ordinary porridge, Ready Brek or a similar oat cereal

** Weetabix or a similar wheat cereal with no added sugar

RECIPES
FOR TODDLERS
FROM
TWELVE
MONTHS
●●●●●●●●●●●●●

Toad 'n' Veg in the Hole

●●●●●●●●●●●●●

4 carrots
1 courgette
8 button mushrooms
30ml (2 tbsp) sunflower oil
3–4 lean beef sausages or vegetarian sausages
125g (4 oz) plain flour
1 egg
300ml (½ pint) milk

Pre-heat the oven to 190°C/375°F/Gas mark 5.

Cut the carrots and courgettes into thick slices. Cut the mushrooms into halves.

Place the vegetables in a roasting tin, drizzle over the sunflower oil and toss to coat.

Prick the sausages. Add to the roasting tin and bake in the oven for 20 minutes.

Meanwhile make the batter. Place the flour, egg and milk in a liquidiser and blend until smooth.

Spoon the roasted vegetables and sausages into a rectangular dish. Pour over the batter and bake for a further 40 minutes until the batter is risen and crisp on the outside.

**MAKES: 2 ADULT AND
2 CHILD PORTIONS**

**STORAGE: 24 HOURS IN THE FRIDGE;
4 WEEKS IN THE FREEZER**

**PREPARATION: 10 MINUTES PLUS
60 MINUTES COOKING TIME**

**NUTRITION: GOOD SOURCE OF PROTEIN,
IRON, CALCIUM, BETA-CAROTENE (VITAMIN A)**

TIP

*This variation of toad-in-the-hole includes vegetables, which add
extra vitamins and fibre to the meal. You can vary the vegetables
according to your child's preferences.*

Healthy Burgers

•••••••••••

175g (6 oz) extra lean minced meat (lamb or beef)
30g (1 oz) dried breadcrumbs
20ml (4 tsp) water
½ onion, roughly chopped
15ml (1 tbsp) fresh parsley, chopped
Freshly ground black pepper
10ml (2 tsp) rapeseed or sunflower oil

Place the minced meat, breadcrumbs, water, onion, herbs and pepper in a bowl. Mix well to combine.

Divide the mixture into 4 balls and flatten into burgers. Heat the oil in a non-stick pan and cook the burgers for 3–4 minutes each side. Alternatively, place the burgers on a baking sheet, brush with the oil and bake in the oven at 200°C/400°F/Gas mark 6 for 10–15 minutes.

Serve in a bap with coleslaw or with home-made chips (see recipe page 204) and peas.

MAKES:
4 SMALL BURGERS

 STORAGE: 24 HOURS IN THE FRIDGE;
4 WEEKS IN THE FREEZER

 PREPARATION: 10 MINUTES PLUS
10–15MINUTES COOKING TIME

 NUTRITION: GOOD SOURCE OF
PROTEIN, IRON, B VITAMINS

TIP

These burgers are made with extra lean meat so they
are much lower in artery-clogging saturated fat than
most bought beef burgers.

Pasta Bolognese

●●●●●●●●●●●●

Bolognese Sauce:
15ml (1 tsp) rapeseed or sunflower oil
1 large onion, chopped
1–2 garlic cloves, crushed
2 sticks of celery, finely chopped
2 carrots, grated
300g (10 oz) lean mince, e.g. beef, turkey
1 tin (400 g) chopped tomatoes
5ml (1 tsp) mixed herbs
Salt and freshly ground black pepper
225g (8 oz) spaghetti or other pasta shapes
(adjust the quantity according to your children's appetite)

Heat the olive oil in a large pan. Add the onions and cook for 3–4 minutes. Add the garlic, celery and carrots and cook for a further 3 minutes until softened.

Add the mince and cook, stirring regularly, until it is browned.

Stir in the chopped tomatoes and herbs. Bring to the boil and simmer for 10 minutes. Season with salt and black pepper.

Meanwhile, cook the pasta according to the directions on the packet. Drain then stir into the Bolognese sauce.

**MAKES: 2 ADULT AND
2 CHILD PORTIONS**

**STORAGE: (SAUCE) 24 HOURS IN THE FRIDGE;
4 WEEKS IN THE FREEZER**

**PREPARATION: 10 MINUTES PLUS
25 MINUTES COOKING TIME**

**NUTRITION: GOOD SOURCE OF PROTEIN, IRON,
BETA-CAROTENE (VITAMIN A), B VITAMINS**

One-pot Chicken Casserole

●●●●●●●●●●●●

30ml (2 tbsp) olive oil
4 chicken thighs
1 onion, chopped
2 garlic cloves, crushed
1 red pepper, chopped
2 carrots, peeled and chopped
125g (4 oz) green beans, chopped
1 tin (400g) chopped tomatoes
15ml (1 tbsp) dried mixed herbs

Pre-heat the oven to 200°C/400°F/Gas mark 6.

Heat 1 tablespoon of the olive oil in a frying pan and sauté the chicken thighs until browned. Remove with a slotted spoon and put in a casserole dish.

Heat the remaining oil. Add the onion and garlic and cook for 3 minutes.

Add the peppers and carrots and cook for a further 2 minutes. Add the beans, tinned tomatoes and herbs and simmer for 5 minutes.

Spoon the vegetable mixture over the chicken then cook in the oven for about 30 minutes.

**MAKES: 2 ADULT AND
2 CHILD PORTIONS**

**STORAGE: 24 HOURS IN THE FRIDGE;
4 WEEKS IN THE FREEZER**

**PREPARATION:10 MINUTES PLUS
45 MINUTES COOKING TIME**

**NUTRITION: GOOD SOURCE OF PROTEIN,
VITAMIN C, BETA-CAROTENE (VITAMIN A)**

Golden Chicken Fingers

●●●●●●●●●●●●

2 chicken breasts, boneless and skinless
60g (2 oz) flour
15ml (1 tbsp) paprika
Salt and freshly ground black pepper
30ml (2 tbsp) olive oil

Pre-heat the oven to 200°C/400°F/Gas mark 6.

Cut the chicken breasts into strips.

Place flour, paprika and seasoning in a plastic bag. Add the chicken strips and shake until the chicken is well coated.

Put the olive oil in a baking dish. Add the chicken strips and turn carefully in the oil. Bake in the oven for 10 minutes until the chicken is cooked and golden brown.

Serve with home-made chips (see recipe page 204) or a baked potato with a green vegetable.

**MAKES: 2 ADULT AND
2 CHILD PORTIONS**

**STORAGE: 24 HOURS IN THE FRIDGE;
4 WEEKS IN THE FREEZER**

**PREPARATION: 10 MINUTES PLUS
10 MINUTES COOKING TIME**

**NUTRITION: GOOD SOURCE OF PROTEIN,
B VITAMINS**

TIP

*Serve these crispy fingers with a dip, such as mayonnaise or
tomato ketchup.*

Home-made Chicken Nuggets

●●●●●●●●●●●●

1 large chicken breast, boneless, skinned
40g (1 1/2 oz) polenta (cornmeal)
2.5ml (1/2 tsp) salt
1.25ml (1/2 tsp) garlic powder
Freshly ground black pepper
90ml (3 fl oz) water
1 egg white

Preheat the oven to 200°C/400°F/Gas mark 6.

Cut up the chicken breast into bite-sized chunks.

Combine the polenta, salt, garlic powder and a little black pepper. Place the mixture in a large plastic bag.

Combine the water and egg white in a bowl. Dip the chicken pieces into the egg mixture, and then drop into the plastic bag. Shake until the chicken is thoroughly coated.

Place the coated chicken pieces on an oiled baking tray. Bake for 10–15 minutes or until tender and golden brown.

Serve with home-made chips (see recipe page 204) or a baked potato with carrots or broccoli

MAKES:
2 CHILD PORTIONS

 STORAGE: 24 HOURS IN THE FRIDGE;
4 WEEKS IN THE FREEZER

 PREPARATION: 10 MINUTES PLUS
10–15 MINUTES COOKING TIME

 NUTRITION: GOOD SOURCE OF
PROTEIN, B VITAMINS

TIP
These home-made chicken nuggets are far healthier than the ready-bought and take-away versions. They are baked rather than fried, reducing the fat content and the need for artificial flavour enhancers.

Chicken Soup

● ● ● ● ● ● ● ● ● ● ● ●

2–3 chicken portions on the bone
2 litres (3.5 pints) water or chicken or vegetable stock
5 carrots, peeled and sliced
1 small turnip, peeled and diced
4 potatoes, peeled and diced
1 leek, trimmed and sliced
4 celery sticks, sliced (optional)
Salt and freshly ground black pepper
30ml (2 tbsp) fresh parsley, chopped

Place the chicken portions, water or stock and the prepared
vegetables in a large saucepan. Bring to the boil, reduce the heat
and simmer for about one hour.

Take out the chicken portions then remove the skin and bones
from the chicken. Chop the meat and add back to the soup. Season
with the salt and pepper.

Simmer for a few more minutes. Serve garnished with chopped
parsley and accompanied with crusty bread.

MAKES: 4 ADULT AND
4 CHILD PORTIONS

STORAGE: 3 DAYS IN THE FRIDGE;
3 MONTHS IN THE FREEZER

PREPARATION: 10 MINUTES PLUS
60 MINUTES COOKING TIME

NUTRITION: GOOD SOURCE OF PROTEIN,
BETA-CAROTENE (VITAMIN A), VITAMIN C, FIBRE

TIP

This is my mum's famous recipe for chicken soup, which I grew up on. It is the best soup in the world, full of goodness and perfect for a winter's day. Make a big pot and it will feed all the family.

Burgers
••••••••••••

15ml (1 tbsp) olive oil
1 small onion, finely chopped
1 stick celery, finely chopped
1 clove garlic, crushed
1 large chicken breast, skinless and boneless
15ml (1 tbsp) fresh parsley, chopped
60g (2 oz) fresh breadcrumbs
Salt and freshly ground black pepper
1 egg yolk
Flour for coating
15ml (1 tbsp) olive oil

Sauté the onion, celery and garlic in the olive oil for 5 minutes.
Meanwhile mince or finely chop the chicken in a food processor.

Combine the onion mixture, chicken, parsley and breadcrumbs in
a bowl. Season with salt and black pepper and bind the mixture
together with the egg yolk.

Form in to 4 mini burgers, roll in flour and sauté in the oil in a
non-stick pan over a medium heat until golden and cooked
through, turning halfway through (about 5–6 minutes each side).

Serve in a bap with tomatoes or with home-made chips
(see recipe page 204) and vegetables.

MAKES:
4 SMALL BURGERS

 STORAGE: 24 HOURS IN THE FRIDGE;
4 WEEKS IN THE FREEZER

 PREPARATION: 10 MINUTES PLUS
10–15 MINUTES COOKING TIME

 NUTRITION: GOOD SOURCE OF
PROTEIN, B VITAMINS

TIP

These are a healthy alternative to beef burgers due to their lower fat content. Unlike traditional burgers, they are fried in only a little oil so they become crispy but not greasy.

Little Meat and Vegetable Parcels

●●●●●●●●●●●●

2 turkey or chicken breasts, skinless and boneless
30ml (2 tbsp) rapeseed or sunflower oil
85g (3 oz) mushrooms, sliced
1 medium courgette, chopped
2 carrots, thinly sliced
10ml (2 tsp) corn flour
200ml (7 fl oz) milk
175g (6 oz) filo pastry

Cut the chicken or turkey into small pieces. Heat 1 tablespoon of the oil in a pan and sauté the meat for 3 minutes.

Add the vegetables and continue cooking for 5–6 minutes until the vegetables are softened.

Stir in the flour. Slowly add the milk, stirring continuously until the sauce has thickened. Remove from the heat.

Cut the pastry into 24 squares each measuring 13cm (5 inches). Lightly brush one square with olive oil, cover with another square and brush with oil. Cover with a third square.

Place a spoonful of the filling in the centre. Brush the edges with a little water. Fold over one corner of the pastry to make a triangle and press to seal. Repeat with the remaining pastry squares until you have 8 parcels.

Place the parcels on a lightly oiled baking tray and brush with olive oil. Bake in the oven for 15–20 minutes until golden brown.

MAKES:
8 PARCELS

STORAGE:
4 WEEKS IN THE FREEZER

**PREPARATION: 10 MINUTES PLUS
30 MINUTES COOKING TIME**

**NUTRITION: GOOD SOURCE OF PROTEIN,
BETA-CAROTENE (VITAMIN A), CARBOHYDRATE**

TIP
*Children love eating little parcels. This recipe uses filo pastry for
the parcels, which is low in fat, but you can use shortcrust or puff
pastry if you like.*

Mini Fish Pies

●●●●●●●●●●●●

300g (10 oz) potatoes, peeled and cut into large chunks
300g (10 oz) swede, peeled and cut into large chunks
550g (1¼ lb) cod fillets
600ml (1 pint) skimmed milk
1 bay leaf
15ml (1 tbsp) butter
2 large leeks, thinly sliced
2 heaped tablespoons plain flour
Salt, freshly ground black pepper, Dijon mustard
60g (2 oz) mature Cheddar, grated

Bring a little water to the boil and cook the potatoes and swede for
about 15 minutes or until soft. Drain and mash with about one
third of the milk.

Meanwhile place the cod in a saucepan with the remaining milk
and bay leaf. Bring to the boil and simmer for about 5 minutes.

Strain the milk into a jug. Roughly flake the fish, carefully removing
any bones.

Melt the butter in a pan, add the leeks and cook for 5 minutes
until softened. Stir in the flour. Slowly add the milk, stirring
continuously until the sauce has thickened. Season with salt,
pepper and Dijon mustard.

Combine the sauce with the leeks and fish. Spoon into four small individual baking dishes, choosing sizes according to the number of adult and toddler portions. Cover evenly with the mashed potatoes and scatter the cheese on top.

Bake at 190°C/375°F/Gas mark 5 for 20 minutes until the top is golden brown.

**MAKES: 2 ADULT AND
2 CHILD PORTIONS**

**STORAGE: 24 HOURS IN THE FRIDGE;
4 WEEKS IN THE FREEZER**

**PREPARATION: 10 MINUTES PLUS
35 MINUTES COOKING TIME**

**NUTRITION: GOOD SOURCE OF PROTEIN,
COMPLEX CARBOHYDRATES, FIBRE, CALCIUM**

TIP

*This popular children's meal is made healthier by adding
swede to the mashed potato.*

Tuna Pasta with Tomato Sauce

•••••••••••••

225g (8 oz) pasta spirals or shells
15ml (1 tbsp) olive oil
1 onion, chopped
1 garlic clove, crushed
1 red or yellow pepper, chopped
1 tin (400g) chopped tomatoes
15ml (1 tbsp) tomato purée
5ml (1 tsp) dried basil
1 x 200g tin tuna in water or brine, drained and flaked
60g (2 oz) Cheddar cheese, grated

Cook the pasta in plenty of boiling water according to the instructions on the packet. Drain.

Meanwhile, sauté the onion and garlic in the olive oil for 3 minutes. Add the peppers and cook for a further 3 minutes. Add the tomatoes, tomato purée and herbs, bring to the boil then simmer for 4–5 minutes.

Add the tuna and heat through. Stir into the cooked pasta.

Spoon into an ovenproof dish, sprinkle the cheese on top and pop under a hot grill for a few minutes until the cheese is melted and golden.

**MAKES: 2 ADULT AND
2 CHILD PORTIONS**

 **STORAGE: 24 HOURS IN THE FRIDGE;
4 WEEKS IN THE FREEZER**

 **PREPARATION:10 MINUTES PLUS
10 MINUTES COOKING TIME**

 **NUTRITION: GOOD SOURCE OF PROTEIN,
COMPLEX CARBOHYDRATES, VITAMIN C**

TIP

*To save time, stir the tuna into a jar of pasta sauce. I like to add
extra peppers and mushrooms.*

Speedy Fish Risotto

●●●●●●●●●●●●

Makes 4 servings
225g (8 oz) easy-cook basmati rice
600ml (1 pint) vegetable stock
(or water plus 2 stock cubes)
1 bay leaf
350g (12 oz) frozen haddock or cod fillets, thawed
200g (7 oz) frozen peas
Salt and freshly ground black pepper

Place the rice in a large pan with the stock and bay leaf and bring to the boil. Cover and simmer for 10 minutes.

Add the haddock and peas and continue cooking for a further 5 minutes until the liquid has been absorbed and the fish flakes easily. Roughly break up the fish and stir the rice mixture to distribute evenly.

- **MAKES: 2 ADULT AND 2 CHILD PORTIONS**
- **STORAGE: 4 WEEKS IN THE FREEZER**
- **PREPARATION: 5 MINUTES PLUS 15 MINUTES COOKING TIME**
- **NUTRITION: GOOD SOURCE OF COMPLEX CARBOHYDRATES, PROTEIN, VITAMIN C, FIBRE**

TIP
Don't re-heat cooked rice that has been stored in the fridge because of the risk of food poisoning. Keep any leftovers in the freezer.

Rosie's Easy Peasy Tuna Pasta

●●●●●●●●●●●●

225g (8 oz) pasta shapes (dried or fresh)
30–45ml (2–3 tbsp) mayonnaise
1 x 200g tin tuna in water or brine, drained and flaked

Cook the pasta in plenty of boiling water according to the instructions on the packet. Drain.

Mix the mayonnaise with the tuna then add to the cooked pasta.

Serve immediately.

MAKES: 2 ADULT AND 2 CHILD PORTIONS

STORAGE: 24 HOURS IN THE FRIDGE; 4 WEEKS IN THE FREEZER

PREPARATION: 5 MINUTES PLUS 10 MINUTES COOKING TIME

NUTRITION: GOOD SOURCE OF PROTEIN, COMPLEX CARBOHYDRATES, VITAMIN E, MONOUNSATURATED FAT

TIP
This dish is one of Rosie's favourites and it's really quick to prepare.

Easy Fish Cakes

•••••••••••••

450g (1 lb) potatoes, peeled
450g (1 lb) salmon or cod fillet
60g (2 oz) butter
60ml (4 tbsp) milk
15ml (1 tbsp) fresh parsley, chopped
Salt and freshly ground black pepper

Cut the potatoes into quarters and boil for 15 minutes until soft.
Drain.

Meanwhile, poach the fish in water for 10 minutes. Drain, skin and
flake the fish, carefully removing all the bones.

Mash the potatoes with the butter, milk, parsley and salt and
pepper. Mix in the flaked fish. Shape into 4 or 8 cakes.

Shallow fry in olive oil for a few minutes on each side. Drain on
kitchen paper.

Serve warm with peas and baked beans.

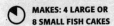

🕐 **MAKES: 4 LARGE OR
8 SMALL FISH CAKES**

❄️ **STORAGE: 24 HOURS IN THE FRIDGE;
4 WEEKS IN THE FREEZER**

🕐 **PREPARATION: 20 MINUTES PLUS
8 MINUTES COOKING TIME**

😊 **NUTRITION: GOOD SOURCE OF ESSENTIAL FATS
(IF USING SALMON), PROTEIN, COMPLEX CARBOHYDRATES**

TIP

*All fish is rich in protein and minerals. Oily fish like salmon
is rich in the essential omega-3 fatty acids, important for
brain development.*

LIGHT MEALS

Vegetable Soup
●●●●●●●●●●●●

30ml (2 tbsp) olive oil
1 onion, chopped
1 garlic clove, crushed
1 red pepper, chopped
2 carrots, chopped
125 g (4 oz) green beans, cut into 2-cm (1/2-inch) lengths
1/2 swede, peeled and diced
1 potato, peeled and chopped
700ml (1 1/2 pints) vegetable stock
(or use 15ml/1 tbsp Swiss bouillon powder and water)
60g (2 oz) small pasta shapes
125g (4 oz) frozen peas

Sauté the onion, garlic and red pepper in the olive oil for 5 minutes.

Add the carrots, beans, swede and potato. Bring to the boil, reduce the heat, cover and simmer for 10 minutes.

Add the pasta shapes and frozen peas and continue to cook for 5 minutes.

Serve as a chunky soup or, for a smooth soup, liquidise in a blender.

Serve with grated cheese and bread.

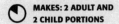 **MAKES: 2 ADULT AND
2 CHILD PORTIONS**

**STORAGE: 3 DAYS IN THE FRIDGE;
3 MONTHS IN THE FREEZER**

**PREPARATION: 10 MINUTES PLUS
20 MINUTES COOKING TIME**

**NUTRITION: GOOD SOURCE OF BETA-CAROTENE
(VITAMIN A), VITAMIN C, FIBRE**

TIP

*Soup is far easier to make than many people think – it's simply a
case of chopping vegetables and putting everything in one pan.
Make a larger quantity and keep the rest in the fridge or freezer.*

Mini Pizzas
•••••••••••••

Making your own pizzas is easy if you have a bread machine. Alternatively, use the quick pizza base recipe or one of the alternative ready-made bases suggested below. If you haven't got time to make your own tomato sauce, use a jar of pasta sauce.

Home-made pizza base:
225g (8 oz) strong white flour
½ sachet easy blend yeast
2.5ml (½ tsp) salt
175ml (6 fl oz) warm water
15ml (1 tbsp) olive oil

If making the dough by hand, mix the flour, yeast and salt in a large bowl. Make a well in the centre and add the oil and half of the water. Stir with a wooden spoon, gradually adding more liquid until you have a pliable dough. Turn the dough out onto a floured surface and knead for about 5 minutes until you have a smooth and elastic dough. Place the dough in a clean lightly oiled bowl, cover with a tea towel and leave in a warm place for about 1 hour or until doubled in size.

If you are using a bread machine, place the ingredients in the tin and follow the instructions supplied with the machine.

Knead the dough briefly. Divide the dough into 8 pieces. Roll each piece into a circle approximately 10 cm (4 inches) diameter.

Transfer the bases on to a couple of oiled baking trays. Let the dough rise for 30 minutes. Spoon on a little tomato sauce (see p 196), scatter over the cheese and any additional toppings (see p 197).

Bake at 220°C/425°F/Gas mark 7 for approximately 10 minutes or until topping is bubbling and the crust golden brown.

Serve with a portion of salad, coleslaw or an extra vegetable.

 MAKES:
8 SMALL PIZZAS

 STORAGE: 24 HOURS IN THE FRIDGE;
4 WEEKS IN THE FREEZER

 PREPARATION: 1½–2 HOURS PLUS
10 MINUTES COOKING TIME

NUTRITION: GOOD SOURCE OF COMPLEX CARBOHYDRATES,
PROTEIN, BETA-CAROTENE (VITAMIN A), VITAMIN C, CALCIUM

QUICK SCONE PIZZA BASE:

225g (8 oz) self-raising white flour
5ml (1 tsp) baking powder
2.5ml (½ tsp) salt
40g (1½ oz) butter or margarine
150ml (5 fl oz) skimmed milk

Mix the flour, baking powder and salt in a bowl.

Rub in the butter or margarine until the mixture resembles breadcrumbs.

Add the milk, mixing quickly with a fork just until the mixture comes together.

Roll or press the dough into 8 circles approx 7cm (3 inches) diameter and transfer onto baking trays.

The base is now ready for topping. Bake at 220°C/425°F/Gas mark 7 for 10 minutes.

TOMATO SAUCE:

15ml (1 tbsp) olive oil
1 small onion, finely chopped
1 garlic clove, crushed
300ml (½ pint) passata (smooth sieved tomatoes)
or 1 x 400 g tin chopped tomatoes
15ml (1 tbsp) tomato purée
5ml (1 tsp) dried basil
2.5ml (½ tsp) sugar
Pinch of salt and freshly ground black pepper

Heat the olive oil in a pan and sauté the onion and garlic for 5
minutes until translucent.

Add the passata or chopped tomatoes, tomato purée, basil, sugar,
salt and pepper. Continue to simmer for 5–10 minutes until the
sauce has thickened a little.

Spread the sauce on the pizza base. Continue with the instructions
given for the pizza bases above.

PIZZA TOPPINGS

This is a good opportunity to add extra vegetables.
Choose as many of the following as you wish:

Cherry tomatoes, halved
Red, yellow and green peppers, sliced
Mushrooms, sliced
Sweetcorn or baby corn
Onion rings
Olives
Courgettes, sliced
Tuna, flaked
Broccoli florets, cooked
Colourful cheeses, e.g. red Leicester, double Gloucester

TIP
Let your children arrange their own toppings, perhaps in the shape of a smiley face or whatever captures their imagination.

ALTERNATIVE READY-MADE PIZZA BASES

Ready-made pizza base
Packet pizza base mix
English muffin, toasted and split horizontally
Mini pitta bread, split horizontally
French bread, sliced in half horizontally

Quick Kiddie Quiches
●●●●●●●●●●●●

200g (¹/₂ pack) ready-rolled shortcrust pastry
60g (2 oz) Cheddar cheese
3 eggs
125ml (4 fl oz) milk
Optional filling ingredients:
Chopped ham
Sliced tomato
Sweetcorn
Chopped peppers
Chopped bacon

Pre-heat the oven to 200°C/400°F/Gas mark 6. Butter or oil 6 holes of a deep muffin tin.

Place the ready-rolled pastry on a floured surface and cut into 6 rounds using an 8-cm (3-inch) cutter. Lightly press into the 6 muffin holes.

Combine the cheese, eggs and milk and pour into the muffin tin. Add any of the optional ingredients (see suggestions above).

Bake in the oven for 20 minutes or until risen and golden. Leave to cool for a few minutes before removing from the tin. Serve warm or cold with baked or mashed potatoes and an extra vegetable.

MAKES:
6 QUICHES

STORAGE: 24 HOURS IN THE FRIDGE;
4 WEEKS IN THE FREEZER

PREPARATION: 10 MINUTES PLUS
20 MINUTES COOKING TIME

NUTRITION: GOOD SOURCE OF PROTEIN,
CALCIUM, COMPLEX CARBOHYDRATES.

TIP
These mini quiches are perfect for picnics and lunch boxes.

Perfect Baked Potatoes
●●●●●●●●●●●●●

Nothing could be easier than baking potatoes. Here's a foolproof guide to ensuring the perfect baked potato.

4 baking potatoes

Pre-heat the oven to 200°C/400°F/Gas mark 6. Wash the potatoes and pierce the skin with a fork. For a crispy skin, rub lightly in a little olive oil before baking. Bake directly on the oven shelf and bake for 30–60 minutes, depending on the size of the potato, or until the flesh is very tender. Cut a cross on the top of each potato, squeeze the sides to open it up and top with any of the toppings below.

TO MICROWAVE POTATOES
Prick the potatoes, wrap each one in absorbent (kitchen) paper. Cook on high for 5–7 minutes for one potato or about 10 minutes for two (timings will depend on the size of the potatoes).

Toppings for baked potatoes:
Cheddar cheese
Tuna mixed with mayonnaise and sweetcorn
Scrambled egg
Hummus
Stir-fried vegetables
Baked beans
Chicken mixed with mayonnaise
Cottage cheese
Ratatouille
Sweetcorn
Bolognese sauce
Full-fat soft cheese or crème fraiche

Best Mash

●●●●●●●●●●●●

450g (1 lb) potatoes, peeled
125g (4 oz) swede, peeled
1 parsnip, peeled
200ml (7 fl oz) milk
Salt, freshly ground black pepper

Cut the potato, swede and parsnip into rough pieces and cook in a little fast-boiling water for 10–15 minutes, until tender. Drain.

Mash the root vegetables with the milk and seasoning. Add a little extra milk for a softer consistency.

GREEN MASH
For a really fun dish, mix mashed potatoes with cooked puréed spinach. It's great to serve on Halloween!

**MAKES: 2 ADULT AND
2 CHILD SERVINGS**

**STORAGE: 24 HOURS IN THE FRIDGE;
4 WEEKS IN THE FREEZER**

**PREPARATION:15 MINUTES PLUS
15 MINUTES COOKING TIME**

**NUTRITION: GOOD SOURCE OF COMPLEX CARBOHYDRATES,
BETA-CAROTENE (VITAMIN A), VITAMIN C, CALCIUM**

TIP
The swede and parsnips add extra vitamins and a subtle sweetness, which children will love.

Sandwiches

●●●●●●●●●●●●

Sandwiches have always been teatime favourites and are perfect for meals on the go. Make them more interesting by varying the type of bread you use. Try wholemeal, oatmeal, mixed grain wheatgerm, raisin or malted grain bread. Remember, white bread doesn't contain as many vitamins, or as much fibre and iron as wholemeal or brown varieties.

Make different shapes, such as triangles or little squares, or use pastry cutters to make circles and stars. Try offering mini pitta breads, little rolls, English muffins, mini bagels and mini baguettes instead of sliced bread.

Here are some ideas for fillings:

Ham, tomato and salad cream

Cheese and peanut butter

Chopped hard-boiled egg and salad cream

Bacon, lettuce and tomato

Cheese and Marmite

Banana and peanut butter

Salmon, mayonnaise and cucumber

Chicken, tomato and mayonnaise

Sardine and cucumber

Tuna, mayonnaise and lettuce

Cream cheese or cheese spread

Hummus (see recipe page 114) and cucumber

Chicken and coleslaw

TIP
Let your children choose their own fillings (even if their combinations seem odd to you!). Older ones will be able to assemble their own sandwiches. Over threes will also be able to spread soft spreads (with a children's knife) and cut sandwiches into interesting shapes.

IT'S A WRAP!

Wraps are a great alternative to the usual sandwich. Soft flour wraps can be found in the bread section of most supermarkets and make perfect wrappings for savoury fillings. Place the filling to the side of the centre of the wrap, fold over the unfilled half then roll up. Cut into 2 to 4 pieces to serve.

Here are some ideas for fillings:
Grated cheese with slices of tomato
Chopped hard-boiled egg or
warm scrambled egg with salad cream
Chopped cooked chicken mixed with
mayonnaise and lettuce
Tuna mixed with mayonnaise and cucumber
Sliced lean ham with tomato and cucumber
Sliced banana and honey

Healthy Home-made Chips

●●●●●●●●●●●●

Deep-fried chips absorb a lot of oil. Here's a version that's healthier and even quicker to prepare. With the skins left on, they retain much of their Vitamin C.

4 medium potatoes, scrubbed (adjust the quantity according to your children's appetite)
20ml (4 tsp) sunflower or olive oil

Preheat the oven to 200°C/400°F/Gas mark 6.

Cut each potato lengthways then cut each half into 6 wedges.

Place in a baking tin and turn in the oil until each piece is lightly coated.

Bake for 35–40 minutes until the potatoes are soft inside and golden brown on the outside.

**MAKES: 2 ADULT AND
2 CHILD SERVINGS**

**STORAGE: 24 HOURS IN THE FRIDGE;
4 WEEKS IN THE FREEZER**

**PREPARATION: 5 MINUTES PLUS
35–40 MINUTES COOKING TIME**

**NUTRITION: GOOD SOURCE OF
COMPLEX CARBOHYDRATES, FIBRE, VITAMIN C**

Snacks on the Move
●●●●●●●●●●●●

When you're on the move with your children, it's tempting to give them quick and easy snacks such as crisps, biscuits and chocolate bars.

Here are some ideas for healthier alternatives:
Apples, grapes, bananas
Small boxes of raisins
Mini packets of dried fruit
Mini breadsticks
Rice cakes and crackers
Fruit bun
Cereal bar
Yoghurt/ fromage frais pouches/ tubes
Individually wrapped mini cheeses
Cheese slices
Cheese snacks (e.g. Strip cheese, cheese strings)
Yoghurt drink

MAIN MEALS WITHOUT MEAT

Vegetarian Spaghetti Bolognese
••••••••••••

15ml (1 tbsp) olive oil
1 onion, chopped
2 carrots, grated
1 x 400g tin chopped tomatoes
225g (8 oz) quorn or soya mince
(rehydrated according to instructions on the packet)
5ml (1 tsp) Swiss vegetable bouillon or
1 vegetable stock cube
5ml (1 tsp) dried mixed herbs
225g (8 oz) spaghetti
30ml (2 tbsp) Parmesan cheese, grated

Heat the oil in a large frying pan. Add the onion and carrots and sauté for 5 minutes until softened.

Add the tomatoes, quorn or soya and herbs. Cook for a further 10 minutes until the sauce thickens slightly.

Meanwhile, cook the spaghetti in boiling water according to the directions on the packet. Drain.

Divide the spaghetti between 4 bowls. Spoon over the Bolognese sauce and sprinkle on the Parmesan cheese.

**MAKES: 2 ADULT AND
2 CHILD SERVINGS**

**STORAGE: 24 HOURS IN THE FRIDGE;
4 WEEKS IN THE FREEZER**

**PREPARATION: 10 MINUTES PLUS
15 MINUTES COOKING TIME**

**NUTRITION: GOOD SOURCE OF COMPLEX CARBOHYDRATES,
PROTEIN, BETA-CAROTENE (VITAMIN A), B VITAMINS**

TIP

*You can use cooked red lentils or a tin (400 g) of lentils instead
of the quorn or soya mince.*

Quick Tomato Pasta
●●●●●●●●●●●●

15ml (1 tbsp) olive oil
1 onion, chopped
1 garlic clove, crushed
1 x 400g tin chopped tomatoes
30ml (2 tbsp) tomato purée
15ml (1 tbsp) dried basil
Salt and freshly ground black pepper
Pinch of sugar
225g (8 oz) pasta shells
85g (3 oz) Cheddar cheese, grated

Heat the olive oil in a large frying pan. Add the onions and garlic and sauté for 5 minutes or until softened.

Add the tinned tomatoes, tomato purée, basil, salt, pepper and sugar. Cook for 5 minutes or until the sauce thickens slightly.

Meanwhile, cook the pasta shells in boiling water according to the directions on the packet. Drain.

Combine the sauce with the pasta. Spoon into 4 dishes and sprinkle over the cheese.

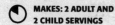 **MAKES: 2 ADULT AND
2 CHILD SERVINGS**

**STORAGE: 24 HOURS IN THE FRIDGE;
4 WEEKS IN THE FREEZER**

**PREPARATION: 10 MINUTES PLUS
10 MINUTES COOKING TIME**

**NUTRITION: GOOD SOURCE OF COMPLEX CARBOHYDRATES,
BETA-CAROTENE (VITAMIN A), PROTEIN**

TIP

*This is one of the easiest stand-by dishes! When you're really
pushed for time, use a jar of pasta sauce. It's also good for hiding
finely chopped or grated vegetables like carrots, mushrooms,
peppers or green beans.*

Marvellous Macaroni Cheese

● ● ● ● ● ● ● ● ● ● ● ●

225g (8 oz) macaroni
60g (2 oz) frozen peas
25g (1 oz) butter
25g (1 oz) flour
300ml (½ pint) milk
2.5ml (½ tsp) Dijon mustard
85g (3 oz) Cheddar cheese, grated
Freshly ground black pepper

Pre-heat the oven to 200°C/400°F/Gas mark 6.

Cook the macaroni in boiling water according to the directions on the packet, adding the frozen peas during the last 3 minutes of cooking time. Drain.

Heat the butter in a pan, add the flour and cook for a minute, stirring continuously. Gradually add the milk, stirring continuously until the sauce just reaches the boil and has thickened.

Remove from the heat, stir in the mustard, half the cheese and freshly ground black pepper to taste.

Stir in the macaroni and peas. Spoon into an ovenproof dish, sprinkle the remaining cheese over the top and bake for 15–20 minutes until the top is bubbling and golden.

**MAKES: 2 ADULT AND
2 CHILD SERVINGS**

**STORAGE: 24 HOURS IN THE FRIDGE;
4 WEEKS IN THE FREEZER**

**PREPARATION: 10 MINUTES PLUS
25–30 MINUTES COOKING TIME**

**NUTRITION: GOOD SOURCE OF
COMPLEX CARBOHYDRATES, PROTEIN, CALCIUM**

TIP

*You can add other vegetables to the cheese sauce – try broccoli
florets, broad beans, carrots or red kidney beans.*

Pasta with Broccoli

•••••••••••••

Makes 4 servings
225g (8 oz) pasta shapes
225g (8 oz) broccoli florets
15ml (1 tbsp) olive oil
1 large onion, sliced
15ml (1 tbsp) corn flour
300ml (½ pint) milk
60g (2 oz) mature Cheddar cheese

Cook the pasta in boiling water according to the directions on the packet. Drain.

Meanwhile, cook the broccoli in a little boiling water for about 5 minutes or until it is just tender but not too soft.

In a non-stick pan, sauté the onion in the olive oil for 5 minutes until softened.

Mix together the corn flour and milk in a jug. Slowly add to the onion, stirring continuously until the sauce has thickened. Stir in half of the cheese.

Combine with the pasta and broccoli. Transfer to a warm serving dish, sprinkle over the remaining cheese and pop under a hot grill until the cheese is melted and golden.

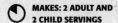

**MAKES: 2 ADULT AND
2 CHILD SERVINGS**

**STORAGE: 24 HOURS IN THE FRIDGE;
4 WEEKS IN THE FREEZER**

**PREPARATION: 10 MINUTES PLUS
10 MINUTES COOKING TIME**

**NUTRITION: GOOD SOURCE OF COMPLEX
CARBOHYDRATES, PROTEIN, VITAMIN C, CALCIUM**

TIP
*Broccoli is full of vitamin C, folate and other powerful
antioxidants. This recipe is a tasty way of getting your
children to eat more broccoli!*

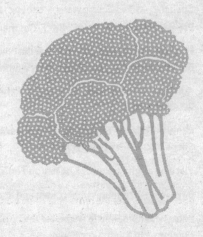

Veggie Burgers

●●●●●●●●●●●●●

15ml (1 tbsp) olive oil
1 small onion, finely chopped
5ml (1 tsp) curry powder
(according to your children's taste)
125g (4 oz) red lentils
400ml (16 fl oz) vegetable stock
85g (3 oz) fresh wholemeal breadcrumbs
Salt and black pepper to taste
A little olive oil for brushing

Pre-heat the oven to 200°C/400°F/Gas mark 6.

Heat the oil in a large pan and cook the onion for 3 minutes.
Stir in the curry powder and cook for a further minute.

Add the lentils and stock. Bring to the boil and simmer for
20–25 minutes.

Allow the mixture to cool slightly then mix in the breadcrumbs.
Shape into 4–6 small burgers.

Place on a lightly oiled baking tray and brush with a little oil.

Bake for 7–10 minutes until golden and firm.

Serve with home-made chips (see recipe page 204) or baked
potatoes and a green vegetable.

MAKES:
4–6 SMALL BURGERS

STORAGE: 24 HOURS IN THE FRIDGE;
4 WEEKS IN THE FREEZER

PREPARATION: 10 MINUTES PLUS
35 MINUTES COOKING TIME

NUTRITION: GOOD SOURCE OF
PROTEIN, IRON, FIBRE, B VITAMINS

TIP

These tasty burgers are made with red lentils, a terrific source of protein, iron and fibre. They are oven-baked using only a little oil.

Vegetables in Cheese Sauce

••••••••••••

2 carrots, peeled and sliced
175g (6 oz) broccoli, cut into florets
175g (6 oz) cauliflower, cut into florets
125g (4 oz) frozen peas
30g (1 oz) butter or margarine
15ml (1 tbsp) corn flour
300ml (½ pint) milk
5ml (1 tsp) mustard
85g (3 oz) mature Cheddar cheese, grated

Cook the carrots in a little boiling water for 5 minutes. Add the broccoli, cauliflower and peas and continue cooking for a further 5–7 minutes under tender. Drain.

Meanwhile, melt the butter in a saucepan. Stir in the flour and cook for 1 minute, stirring continuously. Slowly add the milk, stirring continuously until the sauce has thickened. Mix in the mustard and half of the cheese.

Arrange the vegetables in a baking dish and pour over the sauce. Sprinkle with the remaining cheese. Pop under a hot grill until the cheese is melted and golden brown.

**MAKES: 2 ADULT AND
2 CHILD SERVINGS**

**STORAGE: 24 HOURS IN THE FRIDGE;
4 WEEKS IN THE FREEZER**

**PREPARATION: 10 MINUTES PLUS
15 MINUTES COOKING TIME**

**NUTRITION: GOOD SOURCE OF BETA-CAROTENE,
(VITAMIN A), VITAMIN C, PROTEIN, CALCIUM**

TIP
*This recipe is a terrific way of serving vegetables to children
who do not like them plain. It also works well with sweetcorn,
leeks and courgettes.*

Quick Vegetable Korma

●●●●●●●●●●●●●

1 onion, sliced
15ml (1 tbsp) olive oil
2 carrots, peeled and sliced
125g (4 oz) cauliflower florets
1 courgette, sliced
60g (2 oz) frozen peas
60ml (4 tbsp) water
1 jar (425g) korma sauce

Heat the oil in a large pan and sauté the onion for 5 minutes.

Add the vegetables and water, cover and simmer for 10 minutes or until the vegetables are almost tender.

Stir in the korma sauce and simmer for a further 5 minutes.

MAKES: 2 ADULT AND
2 CHILD SERVINGS

STORAGE: 24 HOURS IN THE FRIDGE;
4 WEEKS IN THE FREEZER

PREPARATION: 10 MINUTES PLUS
15 MINUTES COOKING TIME

NUTRITION: GOOD SOURCE OF BETA-CAROTENE
(VITAMIN A), VITAMIN C, FIBRE

TIP

Korma is a very mild curry – it's creaminess and subtle coconut flavour make it particularly appealing to children so it is a delicious way of getting them to eat their vegetables and introducing them to new flavours! You can use any other variety of curry sauce instead of the korma.

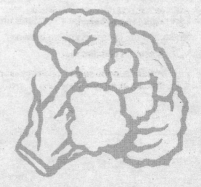

Potato Layer Pie

••••••••••••

450g (1 lb) potatoes, peeled and thinly sliced
2 leeks, thinly sliced
125g (4 oz) broccoli florets
300ml (½ pint) milk
2 large tomatoes, sliced
2 eggs
60g (2 oz) grated cheese
Salt and freshly ground black pepper

Preheat the oven to 200°C/400°F/Gas mark 6.

Arrange half of the potatoes at the bottom of a lightly oiled ovenproof dish. Cover with the sliced leeks, followed by the broccoli and tomatoes. Arrange the remaining potatoes on top and scatter over the grated cheese.

Beat the eggs with the milk, season with salt and pepper, then pour over the pie.

Cover with foil and bake for 45 minutes until the potatoes are tender and the cheese is golden brown.

**MAKES: 2 ADULT AND
2 CHILD SERVINGS**

**STORAGE: 3 DAYS IN THE FRIDGE;
4 WEEKS IN THE FREEZER**

**PREPARATION: 10 MINUTES PLUS
45 MINUTES COOKING TIME**

**NUTRITION: GOOD SOURCE OF COMPLEX
CARBOHYDRATES, PROTEIN, VITAMIN C, CALCIUM**

TIP

*This vegetable pie is really quick to assemble and a good way
of including vegetables in your children's diet.*

Mini Vegetable Pasties

• • • • • • • • • • • •

2 potatoes, peeled and roughly chopped
15ml (1 tbsp) rapeseed or sunflower oil
1 small onion, finely chopped
30ml (2 tbsp) canned sweetcorn (drained)
30ml (2 tbsp) frozen peas
60g (2 oz) Cheddar cheese, grated
1 pack (375g) ready-rolled puff pastry
1 egg, beaten (optional)

Cook the potatoes in a little boiling water for 10–15 minutes or until tender. Drain, then cut into smaller bite-sized pieces.

Meanwhile, heat the oil in a frying pan and cook the onions for 5 minutes until softened.

Remove from the heat. Add the potatoes, sweetcorn, peas and cheese and mix to combine.

Pre-heat the oven to 200°C/400°F/Gas mark 6.

Place the ready-rolled pastry on a floured surface and cut into 8 rounds using a 15-cm (6-inch) cutter or plate as a guide. Brush the edges with a little water. Place a heaped spoonful of the filling in the centres. Bring the edge of the pastry up over the filling and press together firmly to make pasty shapes. Crimp with your fingers. Place the pasties on a baking tray and brush with the beaten egg.

Bake in the oven for about 20 minutes until the pasties are golden. Serve warm or cold.

MAKES:
8 PASTIES

 STORAGE: 24 HOURS IN THE FRIDGE;
4 WEEKS IN THE FREEZER

 PREPARATION: 20 MINUTES PLUS
20 MINUTES COOKING TIME

 NUTRITION: GOOD SOURCE OF COMPLEX
CARBOHYDRATES, PROTEIN, CALCIUM, FIBRE

TIP
You can add other cooked vegetables such as grated carrot, small broccoli or cauliflower florets to the filling instead of the peas and sweetcorn. These pasties are perfect for picnics and lunchboxes.

Vegetable Hot Pot
●●●●●●●●●●●●

15ml (1 tbsp) olive oil
1 onion, chopped
1 garlic clove, crushed
1 red pepper, chopped
6 button mushrooms, chopped
1 courgette, sliced
15ml (1 tbsp) mixed herbs
1 x 400g tin chopped tomatoes
1 x 420g tin mixed beans, drained
1 vegetable stock cube
40g (1 ½ oz) grated Cheddar cheese

Heat the oil in a large pan and sauté the onion for 3–4 minutes
until softened. Add the garlic, red pepper, mushrooms and
courgette and cook for a further 10 minutes.

Add the dried herbs, tomatoes, beans and crumbled stock cube.
Stir well and bring to the boil. Simmer for further 10–15 minutes
until the sauce has thickened.

Spoon in to a baking dish, sprinkle with grated cheese.

Pop the dish under a hot grill for a few minutes until the
cheese is bubbling.

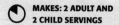 **MAKES: 2 ADULT AND
2 CHILD SERVINGS**

**STORAGE: 3 DAYS IN THE FRIDGE;
4 WEEKS IN THE FREEZER**

**PREPARATION: 10 MINUTES PLUS
25 MINUTES COOKING TIME**

**NUTRITION: GOOD SOURCE OF
COMPLEX PROTEIN, VITAMIN C, FIBRE**

TIP

*This is a really easy one-pot meal. Make a larger quantity and
freeze the remainder.*

Tomato Rice

●●●●●●●●●●●●

Tomato rice is a real hit with Rosie and her friends.

1 tbsp (15 ml) olive oil
1 small onion, finely chopped
1 garlic clove, crushed
225g (8 oz) white or brown rice
1 tin (400 g) chopped tomatoes
450ml ($^3/_4$ pint) vegetable stock
(or water plus 1 vegetable stock cube)
15ml (1 tbsp) tomato purée
5ml (1 tsp) dried basil
60g (2 oz) frozen peas
Pinch of salt and freshly ground black pepper

Sauté the onion and garlic in the olive oil for 5 minutes or until softened.

Add the rice, chopped tomatoes, stock, tomato purée and basil. Bring to the boil, reduce the heat, part cover the pan and simmer for 20 minutes, stirring occasionally, until the rice is tender and the stock has been absorbed.

Stir in the peas and cook for 3 minutes.

Serve with grilled meat or vegetarian sausages and an extra vegetable.

**MAKES: 2 ADULT AND
2 CHILD SERVINGS**

**STORAGE: 24 HOURS IN THE FRIDGE;
4 WEEKS IN THE FREEZER**

**PREPARATION: 10 MINUTES PLUS
25–30 MINUTES COOKING TIME**

**NUTRITION: GOOD SOURCE OF COMPLEX
CARBOHYDRATES, BETA-CAROTENE (VITAMIN A)**

PERFECT PUDDINGS

Raspberry Ice Lollies

●●●●●●●●●●●●

350g (12 oz) raspberries
400ml (14 fl oz) cranberry and raspberry juice drink

Purée the raspberries using a hand blender and pass the mixture through a sieve to remove the seeds. Mix the purée with the cranberry and raspberry juice and pour into ice-lolly moulds.

 MAKES:
8 LOLLIES

 STORAGE:
3 MONTHS IN THE FREEZER

 PREPARATION:
10 MINUTES

 NUTRITION:
GOOD SOURCE OF VITAMIN C

TIP
Home-made lollies are so easy to prepare and much healthier than the bought versions, which are packed with sugar, artificial colours and flavourings. You can buy plastic lolly moulds from kitchen shops and major supermarkets.

Fruit Juice Lollies

●●●●●●●●●●●●

1 litre fruit juice (e.g. orange, pineapple or apple)

Pour the juice into ice-lolly moulds. Once frozen run under the hot tap for a few seconds to remove.

 MAKES:
6 LOLLIES

 STORAGE:
3 MONTHS IN THE FREEZER

 PREPARATION:
5 MINUTES

 NUTRITION:
GOOD SOURCE OF VITAMIN C

TIP
You can make juice lollies with any variety of
fruit juice or even a ready-made smoothie.

Summer Fruit Fool

•••••••••••••

**500g (1 lb) fresh or frozen summer berries
e.g. strawberries, raspberries, blackberries
200g (7 oz) fruit-flavoured fromage frais (e.g. strawberry)
200g (7 oz) Greek yoghurt
15ml (1 tbsp) honey**

Reserve a quarter of the fruit. Mash the remaining fruit with a fork or purée with a hand blender. For younger children, you may also need to pass the mixture through a sieve to remove the seeds.

Mix the fruit with the fromage frais, Greek yoghurt and honey. Spoon in to 4 individual dishes and decorate with the reserved fruit.

 **MAKES: 2 ADULT AND
2 CHILD PORTIONS**

 **STORAGE:
24 HOURS IN THE FRIDGE**

 **PREPARATION:
5–10 MINUTES**

 **NUTRITION: GOOD SOURCE OF
VITAMIN C, FIBRE, PROTEIN**

TIP

You can use other seasonal fruits such as mango, apricots or, in the winter, stewed apples or banana.

Strawberry Frozen Yoghurt

●●●●●●●●●●●●

2 cartons (150 g) strawberry yoghurt
125g (4 oz) strawberries

Purée the strawberries using a hand blender or food processor. Mix in the yoghurt.

Pour into an ice-cream maker and freeze according to the manufacturer's instructions. Alternatively, pour into a plastic container and place in the freezer. When the mixture is frozen around the sides, break up with a fork and mash the ice crystals. Return to the freezer until frozen.

MAKES:
2–3 PORTIONS

STORAGE:
4 WEEKS IN THE FREEZER

PREPARATION:
5 MINUTES

NUTRITION: GOOD SOURCE OF
VITAMIN C, CALCIUM

TIP

Home-made frozen yoghurt is a healthy alternative to bought ice cream and very easy to make. Try using raspberries (sieved), mango, banana or cooked, puréed apricots mixed with a similar flavoured yoghurt.

Banana Ice

●●●●●●●●●●●●

2 ripe bananas

Peel and mash the bananas. Transfer to a small plastic container.

Cover and place in the freezer for several hours.

Allow it to stand at room temperature for 10 minutes before serving.

Serve in bowls or in ice cream cones.

🕐 **MAKES:**
2 CHILD PORTIONS

❄️ **STORAGE: 3 MONTHS IN THE FREEZER;**
DO NOT RE-FREEZE

🕐 **PREPARATION:**
5 MINUTES

😊 **NUTRITION: GOOD SOURCE OF**
FIBRE, VITAMIN C, VITAMIN B6

TIP
Children will enjoy helping to make this ultra-easy 'ice cream'.

Baked Bananas with Chocolate Buttons

●●●●●●●●●●●●

4 bananas
60ml (4 tbsp) water
Chocolate buttons

Preheat the oven to 200°C/400°F/Gas mark 6.

Peel the bananas. Make a slit lengthwise in each banana, not quite cutting all the way through.

Insert the chocolate buttons in the banana slits. Wrap each banana loosely in foil and place on a baking tray.

Bake in the oven for 15 minutes. Unwrap the foil parcels when cool enough and the bananas will be oozing with delicious chocolate sauce!

 MAKES: 2 ADULT AND 2 CHILD PORTIONS

 STORAGE: NOT SUITABLE

 PREPARATION: 15 MINUTES

 NUTRITION: GOOD SOURCE OF VITAMIN C, VITAMIN B6, FIBRE

TIP
This is a good pudding for the children to prepare themselves – that's if they can resist eating all the chocolate buttons first!

Best Apple Crumble

●●●●●●●●●●●●

3 large cooking apples, peeled, quartered and sliced
60ml (4 tbsp) sugar
60g (2 oz) raisins
Pinch of cinnamon (optional)
30ml (2 tbsp) water
125g (4 oz) plain flour
60g (2 oz) butter or margarine
60g (2 oz) sugar

Preheat the oven to 190°C/375°F/Gas mark 5.

Place the apples, sugar, raisins and cinnamon (if using) in a deep baking dish. Combine well and pour over the water.

For the topping, put the flour in a bowl and rub in the butter until the mixture resembles course breadcrumbs. Mix in the sugar. Alternatively, process together in a food processor.

Spoon over the apples. Bake in the oven for 20–25 minutes.

**MAKES: 2 ADULT AND
2 CHILD PORTIONS**

**STORAGE: 3 DAYS IN THE FRIDGE;
4 WEEKS IN THE FREEZER**

**PREPARATION:
15 MINUTES**

**NUTRITION: GOOD SOURCE OF
COMPLEX CARBOHYDRATES, VITAMIN C, FIBRE**

TIPS:

Apple crumble is a firm favourite with Rosie but I have also made super fruit crumbles with tinned apricots, tinned pears, and plums when they are in season and frozen fruits of the forest (a lovely mixture of blackberries, blackcurrants and strawberries).

Apricot Egg Custard

●●●●●●●●●●●●

8 fresh ripe apricots, halved and stoned
3 eggs
70g (2¹/₂ oz) sugar
70g (2 ¹/₂ oz) plain flour
250ml (8 fl oz) milk
5ml (1 tsp) vanilla extract

Preheat the oven to 180°C/350°F/Gas mark 4.

Butter a 1 litre capacity ovenproof glass or ceramic dish.
Arrange the apricots, cut side up, in the bottom of the dish.

Combine the eggs, sugar, flour and milk in a blender.

Pour the batter into the dish and bake for 40–45 minutes
until the custard is golden and set.

Serve warm or cold dusted with icing sugar.

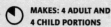 **MAKES: 4 ADULT AND
4 CHILD PORTIONS**

**STORAGE:
3 DAYS IN THE FRIDGE**

**PREPARATION: 10 MINUTES PLUS
40–45 MINUTES COOKING TIME**

**NUTRITION: GOOD SOURCE OF BETA-CAROTENE
(VITAMIN A), FIBRE, PROTEIN, CALCIUM**

TIP

*You can also make this nutritious baked custard with fresh plums,
tinned pitted cherries, sliced pears or pitted prunes.*

DRINKS

Banana Shake

250ml (8 fl oz) milk
2 bananas, sliced
Few crushed ice cubes

Put the milk, crushed ice and banana in a blender.
Whiz until smooth and thick.

MAKES:
2 DRINKS

STORAGE:
NOT SUITABLE

PREPARATION:
5 MINUTES

NUTRITION: GOOD SOURCE OF
VITAMIN C, VITAMIN B6, CALCIUM

Strawberry Shake

● ● ● ● ● ● ● ● ● ● ● ●

150ml (¹/₄ pint) milk
1 x 125g carton low-fat strawberry yoghurt
1 handful of strawberries
Few ice cubes, crushed

Blend together the milk, yoghurt, strawberries and ice in a blender.

 MAKES:
2 DRINKS

 STORAGE:
NOT SUITABLE

 PREPARATION:
5 MINUTES

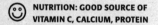 **NUTRITION: GOOD SOURCE OF**
VITAMIN C, CALCIUM, PROTEIN

Berry Shake

225g (8 oz) mixture of fresh or frozen berries,
e.g. raspberries, blueberries, strawberries, blackcurrants
1 carton (150g) fruit yoghurt (e.g. strawberry)
200ml (7 fl oz) milk

Put all the ingredients in a blender and blend until smooth.

MAKES:
2 DRINKS

STORAGE:
NOT SUITABLE

PREPARATION:
5 MINUTES

NUTRITION: GOOD SOURCE OF
VITAMIN C, CALCIUM, PROTEIN

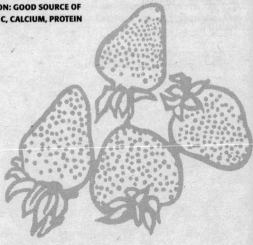

Strawberry and Banana Thickie

••••••••••••

1 handful of strawberries
1 banana
150ml (¼ pint) milk
1 carton (150g) strawberry yoghurt

Put the strawberries, banana, milk and yoghurt in a blender.
Whiz until smooth and thick.

MAKES:
2 DRINKS

STORAGE:
NOT SUITABLE

PREPARATION:
5 MINUTES

NUTRITION: GOOD SOURCE OF
VITAMIN C, CALCIUM, PROTEIN

Raspberry Floats
●●●●●●●●●●●●

2 handfuls of fresh or frozen (defrosted) raspberries
10ml (2 tsp) sugar
125ml (4 fl oz) orange juice
4 scoops vanilla ice cream
Lemonade

Put a handful of raspberries into each of 2 tall tumblers. Add a teaspoon of sugar to each then mash the berries and sugar to a lovely red mush.

Pour some orange juice into each glass. Add 2 scoops of ice cream.

Slowly trickle in the lemonade down the side of the glass and watch it fizz up. Serve with straws.

 MAKES:
2 DRINKS

 STORAGE: UNSUITABLE –
DRINK STRAIGHT AWAY

 PREPARATION:
5 MINUTES

 NUTRITION: GOOD SOURCE OF
VITAMIN C, FIBRE

TIP
This drink is really fun for children to make.

Real Chocolate Milkshake

8 squares of milk chocolate
250ml (8 fl oz) milk
2 scoops vanilla ice cream
6 ice cubes

Melt the chocolate over a pan of simmering water (or microwave for 1¹/₂ minutes).

Mix the warm melted chocolate with 2 tablespoons of milk and stir until thoroughly blended.

Put the remaining milk and chocolate mixture in a blender. Add the ice cream and ice cubes and whiz.

 MAKES:
2 DRINKS

 STORAGE: UNSUITABLE –
DRINK STRAIGHT AWAY

 PREPARATION:
5–10 MINUTES

 NUTRITION: GOOD SOURCE OF
CALCIUM, PROTEIN

TIP
Use plain or milk chocolate for this scrumptious recipe.
Plain chocolate is rich in polyphenols (antioxidants), iron
and magnesium, while milk chocolate contains smaller
amounts of these minerals.

Green Smoothie

●●●●●●●●●●●●

2 kiwi fruit, peeled and roughly chopped
1 large slice of melon, roughly chopped
250ml (8 fl oz) apple juice

Put the fruit blender or food processor and purée. Add the fruit
juice and blend for a few seconds until smooth.

 MAKES:
2 DRINKS

 STORAGE: UNSUITABLE –
DRINK STRAIGHT AWAY

 PREPARATION:
5 MINUTES

 NUTRITION: GOOD SOURCE OF
VITAMIN C, POTASSIUM

TIP
The pale green colour is particularly appealing to
children. Kiwi fruit is an excellent source of Vitamin C
and antioxidants.

Real Lemonade

●●●●●●●●●●●●

4 lemons
85g (3 oz) sugar
1 litre (1.8 pints) water

Using a zester or potato peeler, remove the zest from the
lemons. Place the zest and sugar in a large jug. Squeeze
the juice from the lemons.

Boil the water in the kettle and pour over the lemon zest and
sugar. Stir until the sugar has dissolved, cover and leave to cool.

Add the lemon juice, stir and strain. Chill the drink in the fridge
before serving.

 MAKES:
JUST OVER 1 LITRE

 STORAGE: 3 DAYS
IN THE FRIDGE

 PREPARATION:
10 MINUTES

 NUTRITION: GOOD SOURCE OF
VITAMIN C

TREATS AND SNACKS

Mini Fruit Cakes

• • • • • • • • • • • •

125g (4 oz) sugar
125g (4 oz) butter or margarine
2 eggs
225g (8 oz) white self-raising flour
1.2ml (½ tsp) ground mixed spice
Pinch of salt
90ml (3 fl oz) milk
85g (3 oz) raisins or sultanas

Pre-heat the oven to 200°C/400°F/Gas mark 6. Lightly butter or oil 12 muffin tins or line with 12 paper muffin cases.

Mix the sugar and butter or margarine together until smooth and creamy.

Beat in the eggs then fold in the flour, mixed spice, salt, milk and dried fruit.

Spoon the mixture into the prepared muffin tin. Bake for approximately 15 minutes or until golden brown and firm to the touch.

MAKES:
12 BUNS

STORAGE: 3 DAYS IN AN AIRTIGHT
CONTAINER OR 3 MONTHS IN THE FREEZER

PREPARATION: 10 MINUTES PLUS
15 MINUTES COOKING TIME

NUTRITION: GOOD SOURCE OF
COMPLEX CARBOHYDRATES, FIBRE

TIP
You can add other kinds of dried fruit, such as chopped dates
or cherries instead of the raisins.

Flapjacks

●●●●●●●●●●●●

175g (6 oz) butter or margarine
150g (5 oz) sugar
125g (4 oz) golden syrup
225g (8 oz) rolled oats (porridge oats)

Grease a 15-cm (6-inch) square baking tin. Pre heat the oven
to 180°C/350°F/Gas mark 4.

Put the butter or margarine, sugar and syrup in a heavy-based
saucepan and heat together until melted. Remove from the heat.

Mix in the oats until thoroughly combined.

Transfer the mixture into the prepared tin, level the surface and
bake in the oven for 20–25 minutes until golden brown around
the edges but still soft in the middle.

Leave in the tin to cool. While still warm, score into 12 bars with
a sharp knife.

 MAKES:
12 BARS

 STORAGE: 1 WEEK IN AN AIRTIGHT
CONTAINER OR 3 MONTHS IN THE FREEZER

 PREPARATION: 10 MINUTES PLUS
20–25 MINUTES COOKING TIME

 NUTRITION: GOOD SOURCE OF
SOLUBLE FIBRE, B VITAMINS, IRON

TIP
Oats are highly nutritious and flapjacks are a tasty way of including
them in your children's diet. You can also add a handful of raisins,
chopped glacé cherries or chocolate chips to the oat mixture.

Mini Banana Cakes

●●●●●●●●●●●●

85g (3 oz) soft brown sugar
85g (3 oz) butter or margarine
2 ripe bananas, mashed
1 egg
125ml (4 fl oz) skimmed milk
200g (7 oz) self-raising flour
Pinch of salt
2.5ml (½ tsp) nutmeg

Pre-heat the oven to 190°C/375°F/Gas mark 5. Lightly butter
or oil 12 muffin tins or line with 12 paper muffin cases.

In a bowl, mix together the sugar and butter or margarine.
Mix in the mashed bananas.

Beat in the egg and milk.

Fold in the flour, salt and nutmeg.

Spoon into the prepared muffin tin and bake for about 20 minutes
or until golden brown and firm to the touch.

 MAKES:
12 SMALL CAKES

 STORAGE: 3 DAYS IN AN AIRTIGHT CONTAINER
OR 3 MONTHS IN THE FREEZER

 PREPARATION: 10 MINUTES PLUS
15 MINUTES COOKING TIME

 NUTRITION: GOOD SOURCE OF
CARBOHYDRATE, FIBRE, VITAMIN C

TIP
These little cakes are perfect teatime treats – the bananas add
extra vitamin C and vitamin B6.

Chocolate Chip and Orange Muffins

●●●●●●●●●●●●

250 g (9 oz) self-raising flour
85g (3 oz) sugar
Grated zest of 1 orange
125ml (4 fl oz) orange juice
85ml (3 fl oz) milk
1 egg
85g (3 oz) butter or margarine, melted
85g (3 oz) chocolate chips

Pre heat the oven to 200°C/400°F/Gas mark 6.

Brush a little oil or butter in a muffin tin or line with 12 paper muffin cases.

Mix together the flour and sugar in a large bowl.

Combine the orange zest, juice, milk, egg and melted butter or margarine in a separate bowl. Pour the liquid ingredients into a well in the flour mixture. Mix together.

Add the chocolate chips and combine briefly.

Spoon the mixture into the muffin tin. Bake for about 15 minutes or until risen and golden.

MAKES:
12 MUFFINS

STORAGE: 3 DAYS IN AN AIRTIGHT CONTAINER
OR 3 MONTHS IN THE FREEZER

PREPARATION: 10 MINUTES PLUS
15 MINUTES COOKING TIME

NUTRITION: GOOD SOURCE OF
CARBOHYDRATE

TIP
Chocolate chips are a sure favourite with children but you can
also use dried blueberries, glacé cherries or sultanas.

Pitta Crisps
●●●●●●●●●●●●

2 pitta breads (wholemeal or white)
A little olive oil

Pre heat the oven to 200°C/400°F/Gas mark 6.

Split the pitta breads through the middle and open
out so that you have four halves.

Cut each piece into triangles. Arrange on a baking tray and bake in
the oven for 5–7 minutes until they become crisp and golden.

🕐 **MAKES:**
ABOUT 24

❄ **STORAGE:**
BEST EATEN ON THE SAME DAY

🕐 **PREPARATION: 5 MINUTES PLUS**
5–7 MINUTES COOKING TIME

☺ **NUTRITION: GOOD SOURCE OF COMPLEX**
CARBOHYDRATES, FIBRE (FOR WHOLEMEAL PITTA)

TIP
Children will love these pitta crisps, which are a healthy and tasty
alternative to ordinary crisps. You can sprinkle them with a little
grated cheese halfway through cooking – delicious!

Gingerbread People
●●●●●●●●●●●●

60g (2 oz) butter or margarine
125g (4 oz) soft dark brown sugar
60ml (4 tbsp) golden syrup
225g (8 oz) plain flour
2.5ml (¹/₂ tsp) bicarbonate of soda
10ml (2 tsp) ground ginger
2.5ml (¹/₂ tsp) cinnamon
1 egg

Pre-heat the oven to 190°C/375°F/Gas mark 5. Grease a baking sheet.

Melt the butter or margarine, sugar and syrup in a saucepan.

Add the remaining ingredients and combine quickly to form
a soft dough. If it is too sticky, add a little extra flour.

Roll the dough out on a floured surface, then use a cutter to
make the gingerbread people.

Place on the baking sheet and bake for 10 minutes or until firm
to the touch and golden.

Place on a wire rack to cool. If you wish, you can decorate with icing.

**MAKES: ABOUT 10 (OR MORE
DEPENDING ON THE SIZE OF THE CUTTER)**

**STORAGE: 3 DAYS IN AN AIRTIGHT CONTAINER
OR 3 MONTHS IN THE FREEZER**

**PREPARATION: 10 MINUTES PLUS
10 MINUTES COOKING TIME**

**NUTRITION: GOOD SOURCE
OF CARBOHYDRATE**

INDEX